THE WORLD OF
BATS

THE WORLD OF
BATS

Photographs

NINA LEEN

Text by Alvin Novick

HOLT, RINEHART AND WINSTON

New York · Chicago · San Francisco

Library of Congress Catalog Card Number: 76-84678

First Edition

Some of these photographs previously appeared in *Life* Magazine

SBN: 03-082875-9

Printed in Switzerland

TABLE OF CONTENTS

WHY BATS?

"You can't be serious!" Of course I was serious.

Why the ocean floor, porpoises, Everest, the moon? Why not bats? The most obvious answer was "Because they are there"—and because I got curious about them. We probably know, by now, more about the moon, faraway in outer space, than we know about the uncounted billions of bats, the second largest population of mammals on earth, surrounding us almost everywhere we live.

Only a few years earlier, I got into a panic if I even suspected a flying shadow at dusk to be a bat. I was sure that it was aiming at me and trying to provoke a terrible collision. What would happen to me was never clear in my mind but one thing I was sure of—it would be a frightening experience. It was a fear that I could never logically explain and I know that many thousands of people who still have this fear cannot explain it either. Why should I have felt differently when it was so *natural* to be afraid of bats?

People who would never expect to meet a flamingo in Maine are convinced that they have vampires in their backyards in Connecticut. It is clear that any bat easily becomes a bloodthirsty vampire regardless of behavior or size. Horror movies do not help much either: they do not take the bat image too seriously. When vampires are needed and the real thing is unavailable, the casting problem is simply resolved—close-ups of giant flying foxes with wingspreads of four to five feet play the parts of small, unimpressive vampires. Sadly enough, very few people know the difference. The fact that neither flying foxes from Asia nor vampires from the Western hemisphere roam around the castles of Hungary, Austria or anywhere else in Europe is a small detail never considered important.

My interest in bats began when I was assigned to photograph an essay for the Life Nature Library *Animal Behavior* book. The assignment included a visit with Dr. Donald R. Griffin at the Tropical Research Station in Trinidad. Dr. Griffin was working with bats. With mixed emotions I decided to let fate take its course and hope for the best. Slowly conquering my fear and taking my first close look at a bat's face, I really was shocked, not by its looks but by my own unforgivable stupidity. How could I condemn an animal when I never took the time and trouble to inquire about its looks and its unusual way of life?

What I saw was a mammal with reddish fur (I thought all bats were small and dark) and a face better looking than that of many "unattractive" animals which never frightened anybody! The only startling difference was that this mammal had wings, with the fantastic ability to spread them and take off, landing wherever it wanted to and look down at the super-mammal who, with all his achievements, cannot follow a bat into the air. There is something strangely fascinating in the realization that this creature is unique on earth; there is no other living mammal like it.

I decided to read all about them, their habits, behavior and way of life. It was a surprise to discover how little was published about them. Most bookstores had never even heard of a book about bats. I was able to acquire only three books, but everything in them sounded new to me. Bats emerged as most unusual mammals with built-in capabilities we can only hope to be able to match someday. Even the monstrous faces lost their horror when I found out that the grotesque nose leaves are extremely sophisticated sonar equipment with which the bats are born. It was like discovering a new dimension known only to very few people. Whenever I talked about bats people politely humored me; it was like telling them about the Loch Ness monster. It was hard to visualize bats drinking nectar from flowers or catching fish for a meal. I needed proof, pictures which showed what I was talking about.

I knew that it seemed a hopeless task but I had to try—a few months before, 10,000 bats were destroyed by boys in a cave and maybe it would not have happened if those boys and their parents knew more about bats.

I decided to do whatever I could to get my pictorial proof. I wanted to show that flying and hanging are not all of the bats' way of life, that they climb, jump, swing, swim and walk, that they are colorful, furry and clean. I wanted people to take a close look at these unique animals, to realize that they are different and unknown—not threatening or evil.

To learn more about bats I asked *Life*'s Nature Editor, Patricia Hunt, to lend me material about bats collected in her department. I was able to get some publications from other countries where bats are studied, mostly text with few illustrations. In this way I learned about bats as they have been observed by scientists and naturalists. I made notes of the most interesting information about their looks, their colors, and ways of life—and these became my "picture script" for an essay in *Life* and eventually for this book. It was not my intention to photograph grotesque portraits, but to show the unseen side of bat life—in color.

Considering their importance as natural insecticides, I was not surprised to read that noted scientists, hoping to save them from destruction by ignorant people, have pleaded their case. Several European countries have laws to protect them. Sometimes I am not sure that it is right to disprove the bizarre, foolish superstitions which protect bats from humans. It is true that many have been senselessly tortured and killed, but billions survive undetected because nobody looks for them. I hope nature will protect them from the sad fate of being discovered and slowly made extinct by ruthless "civilized" predators. They coexist without any demands on us; they can afford to ignore us—can we afford to ignore them?

8   — N. L.

AN IMMENSE, OBSCURE DOMAIN

Bats are widely distributed throughout the world. Only in the Antarctic, the Arctic tundra and a few isolated oceanic islands are they unknown. Over 1200 species and subspecies are currently recognized, and there are undoubtedly more to be discovered in parts of the world that have not yet been thoroughly explored.

How many individuals now make up the bat population of the world? The best informed estimate is little better than a guess. To my knowledge only one comprehensive attempt has ever been made to tabulate the bat population of an entire region. This census was limited to one species, the Mexican free-tailed bats. The maximum midsummer cave population in Texas reached about 100 million in 1957, the year the count was made. Judging from this Texas study, from naturalists' reports in Europe and North America, and from my own collecting experience, I might guess the world's bat population to be some tens of billions of individuals.

Nevertheless, many people are only vaguely aware that bats exist. Indeed, numerous North Americans claim never to have seen a bat at all. Most laymen are vaguely afraid of or uncertain about bats and when confronted by one flying in a house or, as often happens, in a summer theater or concert hall, are at least mildly distressed and not uncommonly terrified. Among the first questions which otherwise informed persons ask are: Do they really get in your hair? Do they carry disease? Are they really flying mice or rats? Some just stare with disbelief on hearing that bats are valuable subjects for scientific study.

In fact, bats are interesting and important subjects for scientific investigation for a number of reasons. Their orientation systems provide examples of sonar rivaling manmade designs. We would like to know much more than we do about these beautifully designed sonars. What do bats assess of their surrounding terrain by sending out sound signals and by what features of the returning echoes is information conveyed to them? How is this information

sifted out, coordinated, integrated and acted upon? In order to answer these questions, we must first understand far better than we do the reception and processing of sound by bats' ears and brain centers.

Since bats are mammals, and share physiological mechanisms with other mammals, what we learn of bats can help us to an understanding of how information is processed by the central system, brain and spinal cord, of men. The experimental physiological dissection or step-by-step elucidation of brain function is difficult at best. But through study of a group of organisms having brains so substantially dedicated, as those of bats are, to screening and processing information received in the form of sound, we hope to have the problems somewhat simplified. Because other senses and "higher" centers are limited in bats, they seem likely to lend themselves to experimental procedures better than do more complex mammals such as cats and monkeys. In addition, natural sounds are relatively easily simulated and can be presented to bats in a more natural fashion than can other sensory stimuli to experimental subjects. And we are now equipped with soundproof and echo-absorbing experimental chambers in which we can isolate bats from interference while we guide their attention to such tasks and objects as we wish. For all these reasons and more, bats promise to be useful in elucidating brain and sensory physiology. Our progressing understanding of their sonar systems has already led to discoveries that could help blind people orient themselves.

The next most important contribution bats have to offer as experimental subjects has to do with their temperature regulation. Bats which regularly drop their body temperature to that of the air around them provide a natural laboratory in which to study the influence of temperature on vital mammalian processes such as growth, repair, cell division, molecular replication, and protein synthesis.

Bats also provide an exceptionally wide array of special adaptations of form and function for study by comparative biologists. Analyses of these adaptations—locomotor or renal, respiratory or secretory—often provides us with insight into how animals in general function and evolve.

The longevity of bats, truly astonishing for isolated beings so small, is another absorbing topic for investigation.

Bats come in an unusual variety of species. Among living mammals, their order is second in species only to rodents. They are also potentially highly mobile. Thus studies of their distribution, speciation, and isolation mechanisms will almost surely provide fascinating answers to broad questions of evolution and zoogeography. Their mobility and variety approximate that of birds which have, in these regards, already been exceptionally well studied. A parallel series on bats would enhance the confidence level of the conclusions drawn from earlier studies of birds.

Many interesting peripheral questions also arise. Birds, by their predations, have substantially affected the appearance and behavior of insects. Do insects preyed upon by bats (by acoustic rather than visual means) show parallel developments or evolutionary trends? Answers to the experimental questions which can be raised would have far-reaching and powerful implications.

Finally, among living organisms bats are marvels of compactness and efficiency in the adaptation of their bodies to the special requirements and opportunities of their way of life.

Why so obscure?

How can animals present in the world in such numbers, so widely distributed, offering science so many interesting challenges, be so obscure to so many people?

In the temperate zones bats are relatively sparse both in species and total numbers. Many of them are small, fly only at night, when they are of course hard to see at all, let alone follow for more than a few seconds. They often roost in dark caves which people generally fear to enter. Where people are aware of the presence of bats they often do not welcome them. Bats often roost in attics or barns where their presence may be taken to be a sign of slovenly housekeeping or of tolerance of "vermin."

The obscurity of bats can be further exemplified by considering the vocabulary in English for referring to or naming them. Only a handful of words—bat, vampire, flying fox, and, perhaps, fruit bat—can be described as genuinely in usage. Of these, vampire has an uncertain meaning for many people who consider it to be a nocturnal blood-sucking "spirit" rather than a bat. Flying fox or fruit bat are terms actually known to and used only by travelers and naturalists. Dictionaries also list "flitter mouse" and "reremouse," terms which may still be in use in some parts of the English-speaking world but certainly not in America.

Many bats, of course, have been given "common" names by naturalists or scientists who have hoped thereby to make them better known or more accessible to laymen. Probably all of the English "common" names of bats in non-English-speaking countries, especially non-European countries, are fresh coinages of naturalists. Most species of bats have been endowed with several common names. Even more confusingly, different bats have often been given the same common name; there are no "rules" forbidding this and no international agency exists to clarify usages or to forbid duplication. How many "big-eared" bats there must be!

To get a feel for the interaction of active, everyday vocabulary and the degree of obscurity of this group of animals, consider a comparable group, such as birds. All informed Americans, even those expressing no interest in birds whatsoever, have a basic vocabulary of at least dozens of bird names: owl, hawk, pigeon, sea gull, robin, sparrow, blue jay, warbler, duck, swan, ostrich, and turkey.

THE NATURE OF BATS

Bats are mammals with all the characteristics that mammals share—fur, regulated body temperatures, differentiated teeth, and well-developed nervous systems capable of learning. They also bear their young alive and nourish them with milk. Bats, of course, differ from all other mammals in that they fly. Only three other groups, insects, birds, and the extinct pterosaurs, have evolved true powered flight, though many others glide or soar, depending upon air currents or parachute-like arrangements. All flying animals have and require highly developed neuro-muscular systems, efficient respiratory and circulatory systems, and complex patterns of behavior. Other bat features such as nocturnality, shyness, and small size were apparently common to most of the early placental mammals which had to compete in a world dominated by diurnally active, carnivorous reptiles. Endogenous temperature regulation by the ancestors of bats permitted, perhaps for the first time, a substantial exploitation of nocturnality, thus conferring on them the advantages of being abroad when potential predators were at rest.

In evolution bats derived from a primitive stock of placental mammals, the Insectivora, represented today by such living forms as shrews and hedgehogs. Reconstructions of evolutionary descent are usually based on anatomical similarities and the assemblage of ancestral fossil sequences, but very little in the way of a fossil record of bat ancestry has been discovered.

Analysis of anatomical features of bats, their teeth, their skeletal structure (except those adaptations that are associated with flight), and their organ systems indicate their derivation from primitive and extinct insectivora. Any relationship to rodents is remote. As best one can measure and express these things, bats are more closely allied with Primates, including man. Indeed, early taxonomists grouped bats with Primates in a taxon called Quadrumanes, on the basis of the primitive but versatile development of the limbs and especially the hands and feet. Like Primates, bats often show opposition of the first finger and the first toe and a considerable amount of individual control of the other digits.

ANATOMY

In weight and size bats show great variations. Among the common bats of North America, little brown bats, *Myotis lucifugus*, often weigh about 5 grams (30 grams equal 1 ounce). Their precise weight, of course, varies with time of day, season, and pregnancy. Even smaller are *Pipistrellus subflavus*, the eastern pipistrelles, and *Myotis subulatus*, the small-footed bats. *Eptesicus fuscus*, the big brown bats, and *Tadarida brasiliensis mexicana*, the guano bats, both of which commonly weigh about 12 grams, may be taken to be average-sized in the North American context. *Antrozous*, the pallid bats, *Lasiurus*, the red and hoary bats, and *Lasionycteris*, the silver-tipped bats, are somewhat larger.

Since few bats have been weighed while alive, their size is often represented by the useful index of forearm length, which is easily measured from preserved specimens. Forearms of perhaps 20-36 mm would represent small bats; up to 45 or 50 mm, medium-sized bats. The largest American genera, the tropical *Vampyrum*, *Phyllostomus*, and *Chrotopterus* have forearms of 65-105 mm in length. Adults of *Vampyrum spectrum* weigh up to 190 grams.

The Old World bamboo bat, *Tylonycteris pachypus*, is probably the smallest bat and may well be the smallest living mammal. Individuals of the smallest subspecies weigh about 1.5 grams and have forearms of 21-23 mm. These bats are truly tiny: when I placed one with its wings folded on the terminal joint of my thumb, it was framed on all sides by a substantial margin of my skin. Consider the compactness and efficiency of such an organism—to have all of the mammalian organs, digestive tract, liver, heart, lungs, brain, reproductive system, kidneys, blood, bones and musculature, plus a pair of wings, and to weigh only 1.5 grams.

Probably the largest of the suborder Microchiroptera in the Old World are *Cheiromeles*, the naked free-tailed bats,

which weigh up to 250 grams, and the giant hipposiderids, with forearms of up to 105 mm. Among the suborder Megachiroptera some members of the genus *Pteropus* weigh as much as 900 grams, have forearms of 225 mm and wing spreads of over 1.5 meters. At the other extreme, the tiny flower-feeding genera such as *Macroglossus* have forearms of about 40 mm.

What establishes or governs the size of bats? A number of factors undoubtedly compete. Obviously increased weight means increased flight load. However, larger size also makes for efficiency of temperature regulation and allows for greater reserves of fat to cover short periods of bad weather or food scarcity. A larger bat may also be better able to defend itself against predators; on the other hand, it may make it a more tempting or more obvious target. Flying foxes, for example, are large enough to be worth pursuing and are widely eaten by man.

Larger bats, of course, require more food. Most of the large species are frugivorous; a few are carnivorous or omnivorous. Only *Cheiromeles* and the larger hipposiderids among the heavier species are insectivorous. On the other hand, the smallest bats are insectivorous or flower feeding. Distinguishing cause and effect in correlations of this kind can be very difficult. Perhaps large size facilitates collecting fruit, penetrating thick skin or carrying pieces of fruit to a safe roost for consumption. Similar considerations might apply to carnivorous bats. There may, on the other hand, be an optimal size for feeding on the average insects of the night air. A large bat, for example, may not be able to maneuver efficiently. Or it might be restricted to high altitudes and therefore have to depend upon a year-round supply of high-altitude insects on which to prey.

Small size undoubtedly confers the opportunity of using as shelters small caves, crevices, or caves with narrow entrances. Large size may optimize escape potential; small size increases obscurity. A large number of small bats occupying a niche may be more efficient at capturing prey than a few large individuals would be.

Except for its wings, in flight, the most conspicuous part of a bat is its head. Bat faces and ears are designed in unusual fashions. Flying foxes and many of the pteropodid relatives have the most "normal" faces—large, typically mammalian eyes; small, attractive ears; and rather dog- or foxlike muzzles. Among the flower-feeding pteropodids muzzle length is exaggerated. In males of the pteropodid genus, *Hypsignathus*, which are solitary and inhabit the African rain forest, the muzzle is grotesquely horselike. Male *Hypsignathus* also possess an extraordinarily well-developed larynx which extends down into their abdomen as far as the navel and fills about one-fifth of their body cavity. It functions in producing an apparently social call. Species and sex-recognition signals are undoubtedly

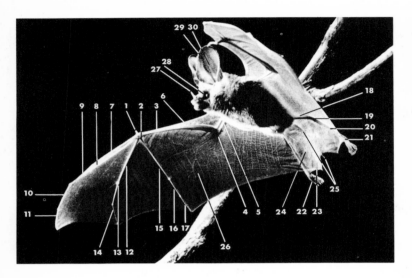

1. Thumb — 2. Wrist — 3. Forearm — 4. Elbow — 5. Upper arm — 6. Extension of wing anterior to arm — 7. Second finger (elongate metacarpal and very short phalanges) — 8. Third metacarpal — 9. First phalanx of third finger — 10. Second phalanx of third finger — 11. Terminal phalanx of third finger — 12. Fourth metacarpal — 13. and 14. Phalanges of fourth finger — 15. Fifth metacarpal — 16. and 17. Phalanges of fifth finger — 18. Upper leg — 19. Knee — 20. Lower leg — 21. Ankle — 22. Foot — 23. Heel bone — 24. Interfemoral membrane — 25. Tail — 26. Wing membrane — 27. Nose leaf — 28. Eye — 29. Pinna (external ear) — 30. Tragus (external ear)

Hypsignathus monstrosus (male). The enormous, peculiar muzzle and lips (with capacious cheek pouches) may be used for manipulating juicy fruit. Adult males are said to produce bell-like "kwok's" every second throughout the night.

Megachiropteran eyes. In these bats, such as *Rousettus*, ▶ the eye is large, generally protuberant, and has a well developed, active iris.

important in solitary bats and the superlarynx of *Hypsignathus* may be needed for the sound-generating power required for communication in the dense jungle canopy.

In the Megachiroptera, the eyes are not only large but are also protuberant. The iris, usually brown, is well developed and reacts well to light. Most of these bats roost outdoors and lack sonar so that, like other mammals, they depend on vision for a variety of functions. Their retina is thrown into curious ridges and valleys which may be an adaptation for vision in faint light.

In the Microchiroptera, the eyes are often exceedingly small. In many molossids, and in *Natalus* and *Chilonycteris*, laymen often fail at first to find the eye. In others, such as *Macrotus*, the eye is rather large and obvious. Unfortunately, we know little about the function of eyes in the Microchiroptera. If cave seclusion during the day is important to the survival of bats and/or nocturnal feeding is advantageous, then it becomes important for bats to be able to distinguish day from night and to synchronize their activities with the ambient light. The best way to do this obviously is to use a light detector. Thus, even if eyes

in bats are obsolete for other reasons, they may well have been preserved for distinguishing day from night.

Among the Microchiroptera, the ears are generally large and often rather funnel-shaped. The pinna is enlarged, as may also be the tragus or antitragus, conspicuously guarding the entrance to the ear canal. Generally bats' ears are very mobile and some appear to be in continual flicking motion while the bat is inspecting its environment. Such ear movements in horseshoe bats have been shown to alternate with and to correlate well with the emission of orientation pulses. These ear movements may aid in echolocation of targets.

In molossids, the ears are fixed or relatively fixed in position and shaped startlingly differently from those of other bats. They often meet and fuse across the midline as do those of the false vampires such as *Megaderma*. In two heavily furred but unrelated genera, *Mormoops* and *Lasiurus*, the ears appear to be countersunk into the fur, or pelage. Unfortunately we know almost nothing of the meaning of these variations. The ears are known to be highly directional in their sensitivity and the pinna and

Tadarida molossa ears. Fused across the ▶
midline and relatively immobile, they
give the impression of a hat or super-
structure. Indeed, the face seems to
consist of snout and ears alone.

Microchiropteran eyes. These are usually
small and often show up poorly against dark
or dense fur. In *Phyllonycteris aphylla*, the
Jamaican flower bat, the eye is clearly
visible in spite of its size.

Euderma ears. Few bats have ears as well
developed as those of the spotted bat and
its relatives. The enormous pinna can be
partly folded away by a series of pleats
into a ram's-horn shape or it may be
held completely erect.

Molossid ears: In *Molossus rufus nigricans* rather small but strikingly peculiar in design. ▶

tragus have been shown to be responsible for a substantial
portion of this directionality.

Many families of bats have rather unexceptional-looking
nostrils. Others have evolved a nose leaf which surrounds
the nostrils and projects above them. Not only have nose
leaves evolved separately at least three times but they are
so elaborate and species-characteristic as to assure us of
their importance. In general, bats that have a nose leaf
emit their sonar pulses through their nose. Those without
a nose leaf generally emit their pulses orally. Furthermore,
F.P. Möhres and his colleagues at Tübingen University
have shown that the nose leaf serves to beam the sound
output of horseshoe bats. Unfortunately, other attempts
to study the function of the nose leaf have been un-
productive.

A bat's mouth is generally large and well provided with
multi-cusped teeth. A full quota of teeth numbers 38 but
many genera have fewer. The vampire, for example, with
20 highly modified teeth, has the smallest count.

The teeth of insectivorous bats are designed for cutting
up the chitinous exoskeletons of their prey, rapidly reducing
them to the consistency of a lumpy pudding. In some
cases bats chew their prey less thoroughly at first and
temporarily store the fragments in the cheeks, later
rechewing and swallowing them. In frugivorous bats, the
much-flatter teeth appear to be designed more for a grind-
ing and extracting action.

A bat's body has the same regions that characterize all
mammals—head, neck, chest, abdomen, and tail. The
neck is mobile but not as conspicuous as it is in birds, whose
head and beak often serve to manipulate objects. Bats do
not manipulate food or other objects very much and when
they do so they often use their feet.

The chest is usually the bulky part of the bat. Not only
does it house most of the powerful wing musculature, but
the hips, being little used in walking or in supporting
weight, are slim in contrast. Their resulting shape—thin
hips and robust chest and shoulders—sometimes makes
them hard to hold on to.

The anatomy of the wings is described in detail in a
separate chapter. The wings are simply modified forelimbs
with webbing that extends not only between the fingers

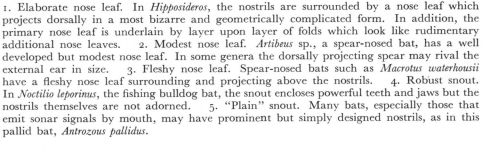

1. Elaborate nose leaf. In *Hipposideros*, the nostrils are surrounded by a nose leaf which projects dorsally in a most bizarre and geometrically complicated form. In addition, the primary nose leaf is underlain by layer upon layer of folds which look like rudimentary additional nose leaves.   2. Modest nose leaf. *Artibeus* sp., a spear-nosed bat, has a well developed but modest nose leaf. In some genera the dorsally projecting spear may rival the external ear in size.   3. Fleshy nose leaf. Spear-nosed bats such as *Macrotus waterhousii* have a fleshy nose leaf surrounding and projecting above the nostrils.   4. Robust snout. In *Noctilio leporinus*, the fishing bulldog bat, the snout encloses powerful teeth and jaws but the nostrils themselves are not adorned.   5. "Plain" snout. Many bats, especially those that emit sonar signals by mouth, may have prominent but simply designed nostrils, as in this pallid bat, *Antrozous pallidus*.

but from the upper arms, forearm, and fifth finger to and along the side of the body to the foot or ankle.

We know relatively little of the internal anatomy of bats. Their digestive tract is usually quite short and, except in the vampires, seems not to be particularly specialized. No bat takes long to digest its food; none feeds on foods which require highly specialized processing, such as grass or browse. Insectivorous or carnivorous bats chew their food so thoroughly that the particles are well exposed to digestive enzymes as soon as they are swallowed. Many of the frugivorous species, if not all, chew their food equally well and often spit out the pulp, swallowing only the juice. Flower feeders, of course, subsist largely on nectar, a food which is already in solution, and on pollen, which is in very small particles. Since chemical digestion proceeds quickly, great intestinal length is not required. There is little residual and what little there is is rapidly ejected. A bat's intestines, therefore, do not harbor a rich bacterial flora.

Only a few surface features appear on bats. Female bats, of course, have mammary glands. These are usually axillary, one on each side, high on the chest and somewhat under the arm. Some genera of bats also have false inguinal nipples which the young use as anchor points when they are not feeding.

In males, the testes, normally intra-abdominal, descend to the scrotum at the beginning of the short reproductive season. Seasonal descent of the testes is common in mammals, more common, in fact, than permanently scrotal testes. Viable sperm is produced by mammals (with a few exceptions) only when the testes are cooler than the usual mammalian body temperature. The scrotal position allows for such cooling. Scrotal testes are, however, vulnerable to injury, and in bats may alter the center of gravity in terms of flight mechanics.

The body ends posteriorly with the tail. This is one of the most variable anatomical features. Tail anatomy and function are often complicated by the presence of an interfemoral membrane, similar in substance and appearance to the wing membrane, extending between and supported laterally by the legs. The interfemoral membrane may be supported in its midline by the tail.

The interfemoral membrane is developed particularly well in insectivorous and carnivorous species. It seems to serve them principally as a basket into which large prey can be thrust during flight while the bat readjusts its tooth-hold. The interfemoral membrane probably also functions in some flight maneuvers but it cannot be a great advantage here since it is absent in many frugivorous and flower-feeding genera.

Euderma teeth. In the spotted bat, the dagger-like canines and the multicusped cheek teeth are designed for holding large insects or other arthropods while also cutting them into tiny fragments.

In several families of bats—the vespertilionids, for example—the tail is very long and runs the length of the interfemoral membrane. In flight, the tail governs the posture of the membrane and at the roost the tail furls the membrane to some extent. In these forms, then, the tail and the interfemoral membrane are integrated in function. In freetailed bats, the tail extends beyond the interfemoral membrane. When this bat is at rest with legs flexed, the membrane slides up along the tail (the skin is only loosely affixed to it) and falls into loose folds. The free tail points backwards or backwards and upwards. Since these bats often roost in crevices and appear to prefer roosting in body contact with stone or building components or with each other, and since they often back into their crevices, I believe that the tail (and the hairs on the feet) may serve a tactile or probing function. The tail may serve a similar function in the mouse-tailed bats.

In the sheath-tailed bats, the tail about halfway along the interfemoral membrane pokes into a dorsally-projecting sheath. In flight, the tail slips out of the sheath and supports the membrane. At rest, the membrane folds at the origin of the sheath and the tail points conspicuously but for no known reason dorsally and posteriorly. Among the spear-nosed bats, the tail may be well developed, totally absent, or almost anywhere in between.

Noctilio leporinus teeth. In the fishing bulldog bat *(above, left)* the large canines are used for holding fish in flight and perhaps for piercing and killing them. The sturdy, cusped cheek teeth are used for reducing the prey to fragments. Fruit bats' teeth are shown at right above. In flying foxes the blunt cheek teeth grind fruit and express the juice. The long, papillated tongue is used to "worry" away fruit pulp by abrasive licking.

◄ *Hipposideros* body proportions: head and shoulders large, neck short, hips slim. Vampire thumbs *(below)* are somewhat elongated and have a series of pads on the undersurface. ▼

The axillary position of the mammary gland of *Leptonycteris sanborni* can be seen below as she balances on the edge of a cactus flower.

Interfemoral membrane of *Noctilio leporinus*. In the fishing bulldog ▶ bat this membrane is particularly full and basket-like.

Whiskered feet of *Tadarida molossa*. Free-tailed bats may use their whiskered feet and long tail for probing the roost or for assessing their position and contact with the roost or with other bats. These bats normally occupy tight spaces in contact with rocky crevice walls, structural components, or with colleagues, where inspection in the dark cannot conveniently be done by echolocation. ▼

Fur-covered *Lasiurus cinereus*. The dorsal surface of the interfemoral membrane and the tail of the hoary bat are completely covered with fur.

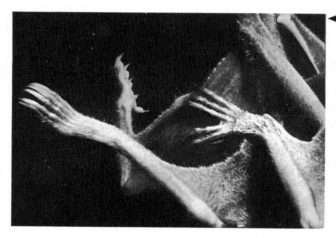

◀ Vampire feet and claws. These are designed not only for grasping a secure hold on a rocky or wooden roost but for walking gently up to or across a sleeping animal. Two of the feet seen here demonstrate the opposability of the toes, showing a partition of action between the third and fourth toes.

Noctilio feet. In the fishing bull- ▶ dog bat, the feet are exceptionally large and powerful. The claws are sturdy, well curved, and sharp for gaffing and carrying fish. (The fifth toe is invisible here.)

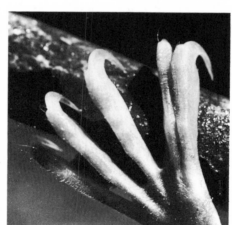

The feet in bats always have five toes with well developed claws that are used for hanging, the normal roosting position for many bats. The toes lie side by side but can be spread and moved individually. In some genera, *Cynopterus* for example, one foot may be used to hold a morsel of fruit, pending eating or between nibbles, while the other foot is engaged in holding on to the roost. In many genera of bats, if indeed not all, the feet (one at a time) are used for combing the fur and for grooming and scratching generally.

In all bats, the toe claws are almost semicircular and sharp, making it possible for them to grasp secure roostholds. Bats do not scratch aggressively or otherwise use their toe claws in defense. In a few genera, though, the thumb claws are used for defense. In *Pteropus* the thumb is particularly well developed and provided with a sturdy

claw. (Some years ago, I borrowed a single male *Pteropus giganteus* from the Dehiwela Zoo in Colombo, Ceylon, to determine whether it was able to orient acoustically. One aspect of its behavior proved to be startling. When I attempted to take it from its cage, the bat kept striking at my hands with its sharp thumb claws as well as with its full set of impressive teeth. I despaired of getting any cooperation; my leather gloves were obviously too flimsy to protect me. Finally I thought of wrapping my hands in some heavy cotton nets. To my surprise, the bat showed no aggressiveness whatsoever toward wrapped hands and allowed me not only to take it from its cage but to continue to work with it without further ado. What could have been the significance of this behavior? Seemingly the bat was frightened by hand- or finger-shaped objects. Was this natural? Or did the bat learn something during its stay in the zoo? Had a keeper threatened or teased the bat with his hands?)

With the exception of the naked free-tailed bat, the skin of bats is covered with fur. In some groups, free-tailed bats and flower bats among them, the fur is short and plush- or velvetlike. In others, some horseshoe bats, the hoary bat, or the big brown bat, *Eptesicus*, the fur is quite long and full.

Many bats have a beautiful pelage. Most come in shades of brown and tan but even these are colorful in good light, the brown often being metallic, cinnamon, or ochraceous. Black and dark mahogany are not uncommon, especially among freetailed bats. Juveniles in many groups are darker than their parents and tend to have grayish tones. The most common color variants in brown or black species are toward auburn, red, or orange. Yellow, maize, and beige occur as well, particularly on the ventral surface. Several white bats are also known. Here and there, striking, unlikely white markings occur, as in *Euderma*, the spotted bat. Otherwise-black or brown bats often show patches or ruffs of red or orange around the neck, shoulders, or throat. White or beige stripes or spots often appear on the face (around the eyes in some pteropodids), the back, or the shoulders. Some, *Rhynchonycteris* and *Nyctimene* for example, are spattered or flecked all over with one or several different colors.

The fur on the throat, neck, or shoulders may be longer or of a different texture from the rest of the fur so as to convey the impression of a ruff. In many genera, a large dermal gland is associated with such differentiated fur. The secretion in some has a musky odor but in others no odor is apparent to man. Dermal glands may be found not only on the throat but on the face, at the edge of the wing, or near the anus as well. The glands often open into a normally furred but invaginated sac of skin and the secretions coat this partially hidden fur. Presumably the sac can be everted, or at least held open, and perhaps the fur is rubbed on landmarks at the roost or on to the feet or claws. We do not know how these glands function. In many other mammals secretions of this kind are used as species- or sex-recognition signals or as territorial markers. Dermal secretions, of course, are also used in many mammals for dressing and conditioning fur and skin.

BAT WAYS OF LIFE

The governing features of the bat way of life are two: flight and nocturnality. Flight facilitates exploitation of food sources at a distance from the roost while allowing large aggregates of individuals to live at the same roost. Flight also permits efficient utilization of flying or roosting insect-populations or large concentrations of fruit and flowers. Each of these food sources is exploited by other animals using other mechanisms but not as efficiently as they are by bats using echolocation.

Nocturnality not only provides security from predators but probably also confers some physiological advantages on bats. Bats seem to have evolved in the tropics and, indeed, most are still confined to the tropics. Diurnal flight in the tropics, unless restricted to the jungle canopy or its shade, would mean exposure of the thin wing membranes to ultraviolet and infrared radiation and to dehydration. We lack data on heat production and loss in flying bats but we can guess that the extensive surface of the wings would absorb heat rather than dissipate it in diurnal, sun-exposed flight. In addition, the air temperature is high enough during the day in many parts of the tropics to preclude much heat loss by convection or reradiation. Heat loss, therefore, might depend on the vaporization of water. Carrying water for vaporization would mean an increased flight load without an ultimate gain. Also, replenishing water for vaporization would mean staying within range of suitable water sources and would thereby restrict the choice of feeding territories. At night, the heat generated by flight is more easily dissipated and water need not be used for temperature regulation.

The dividend of nocturnality

The most important feature of nocturnality, however, is that it makes an enormous, almost exclusive food-supply available—night-flying insects.

Representatives of four families, the vespertilionids, the free-tailed, the spear-nosed, and the horseshoe bats, occupy parts of the temperate zone, but only the vespertilionids have become widely established. Many vespertilionid genera, both tropical and temperate, are truly worldwide. Among the molossids, a few species venture well into the temperate zone but do so as a rule only seasonally. The same is true of the spear-nosed bats. Several European and Asiatic horseshoe bats seem well adapted to temperate climates the year round.

A tropical habitat presumably has the advantage of affording a year-round food supply, whether this be insects, fruit, or flowers. In addition, nocturnal temperature, humidity, and weather in some tropical regions are relatively stable even though there are, of course, seasonal cycles. Even in the tropics, however, habitats vary. At high altitudes, and in dry regions, the bat fauna drops off.

Among the problems that have to be solved by bats colonizing temperate countries are the shortage of food during winter and the challenge of winter temperatures and weather. In addition, summer nights are short compared with those of the tropics so feeding must perhaps be more efficient or more hurried. Night temperatures are not necessarily lower than those in the tropics but are likely to be more varied.

Most of the guano bats that live in the southwest of the United States in the summer migrate south into central Mexico for the winter. The advantages of having separate summer and winter habitats must be substantial to be worth a 1500 mile (2500 km) flight twice a year. Uncertainties of food supply and weather must claim a portion of the population on migratory flights and, in any event, a lot of energy is spent on what is not obviously immediately productive travel. Many red and hoary bats of North America spend the summer in the northern states and Canada but migrate south to Georgia, Alabama, and the Carolinas in the fall. The advantage in these annual migrations may come from spreading the population into areas of otherwise unexploited food-supply and doing so during pregnancy and lactation. Migrating bats must have physiological mechanisms to guide their seasonal flights, to store or provide energy for them, and to trigger the flights at the correct time of year.

Migrations are probably set off by day length, which is characteristic of the seasons and is probably monitored by the bat's brain via the eye. Bats that roost in dark caves seem to fly past the entrance before dusk to check the time of day. These flights may synchronize their internal clock with the solar cycle. In most animals on which adequate data have been collected, breeding seasons in both males and females are cyclical and synchronized with the seasons. Day length is usually the synchronizing cue and the same may be true of bats.

The choice of migratory direction is at the moment presumed to be inherited. We do not know to what extent bats migrate together and we do not know if they can find their way, individually, along ancestral pathways. The information could be conveyed culturally to young bats following their elders but there is some evidence from Australian studies that this is not necessarily the case. I would guess that their choice of direction is genetically determined and is subject to physiological influences which indicate southern flight in the fall and northern flight in the spring. But how does a bat that feels driven to fly south identify which way *is* south? We do not know. Visual assessment of the sun, the moon, or the constellations can provide such information when the time of day is known (from the internal clock) but we do not now have evidence that such visual assessments can be or are made. Recent evidence from Donald R. Griffin's laboratory in Trinidad supports the hypothesis that some bats navigate over long distances by vision. *Phyllostomus hastatus*, a spear-nosed bat, home more efficiently, it was found, when allowed full exercise of vision than when blinded or blindfolded. In these cases, the bats may be identifying familiar major landmarks such as mountain ranges or watersheds and orienting relative to them.

At the end of a migratory flight the goal must of course be identified, so as to avoid going too far or stopping short of suitable terrain. The adequacy of the goal probably cannot simply be tested empirically by stopping and trying a series of places. What is suitable in November could easily be unsuitable in January. In fact, bats seem to stop at locations that *are* suitable for the entire season, but we do not know how they recognize these regions.

Species of several genera of bats, *Myotis*, *Eptesicus*, *Pipistrellus*, *Plecotus*, and *Rhinolophus*, live out their lives in temperate regions. They feed during the warm months, store energy in the autumn as fat, and hibernate during the winter. Even in Europa and North America only a small part of the bat population has been studied adequately to track their movements and only a small part of this minority group has been traced through the seasons. Many bats simply disappear in winter and we assume that they hibernate in crevices in caves or cliff faces, in animal burrows, or in the interstices of buildings. Many, however, cluster in open chambers of special hibernation caves which seem to be selected for low air-movement, stable temperatures above freezing, and high humidity. These bats overwinter on stored fat (often equal to lean body weight or more) by sacrificing body-temperature regulation and eliminating all but essential activities. Not only is energy conserved which would otherwise be used in maintaining an elevated body-temperature but the activities of the various organs are also slowed down by cooling. Growth and repair are largely suspended. Digestion and absorption are of course eliminated since feeding is suspended. The heart beats very slowly and respiration is slow and intermittent since tissue needs are low. Even the brain is largely "turned-off" except for sensory alerting systems which respond to intrusions or to excessive cold or heat. Kidney function is also turned down since relatively little regulation of water, ions, or nitrogenous products is required. Intermittent arousals do occur, perhaps to fulfill some physiological need.

Hibernation and reproduction

Reproduction in all hibernating bats is probably highly specialized since the demands imposed by their cyclical life are severe. Females of hibernating species produce their young in the spring and exploit the seasonal abundance of food to support their pregnancy and lactation. The young require some months in which to reach adult stature before cold again sets in. If pregnancy were to occur too early, the mother would be hibernating and unable to afford the metabolic demands placed on her or she would be forced to emerge and forage when food was sparse or absent. Ideally then, pregnancy should begin at the time of maternal emergence from hibernation when the spring flood of insects is on the land. But that would require that males engage in metabolically expensive spermatogenesis and courtship in late winter, when they are barely surviving on stored fat. Instead, bats of hibernating species court and mate in the fall when they are at their nutritional peak. Sperm may then be stored in the female genital tract over the winter, with fertilization and implantation occurring in the spring, or fertilization may occur in the fall but implantation and development may be delayed until spring.

In general, bats bear only one young at a time. A few temperate species, however, do have multiple births. The North American big brown bat, *Eptesicus*, often has twins in part of its range and the red and hoary bats may have triplets or quadruplets. We do not know what proportion of each litter survives. Some tropical species apparently bear young twice a year. All in all, birth rates can be assumed to be roughly one or two young per year per adult female. Sexual maturity probably occurs in some species at one year and in some others at two. Data are sparse.

The death rate is high during the first year. In addition, not all females are fertile, and some proportion of the pregnancies is miscarried. Other young are malformed at birth and quickly succumb. In addition, babies often die of accidents (falls from the ceiling, for example) or disease, predation, or infestation by parasites. In many populations, probably less than half the young reach maturity each year. Knowing of this high infant mortality and of the low reproductive rate, we may predict that the adults cannot be very vulnerable to predators, disease, or weather. Indeed, this seems to be the case. Adult bats have long lives. Several banded North American vespertilionids have been recovered at over 20 years of age. Two, found after death, had lived at least 24 years. Average life spans of temperate bats may be six, eight, or ten years. Discounting infant mortality, common longevity may prove to be 15 or 18 years or more! We do not know how to account for this extraordinary feat. Other small mammals such as shrews or mice may have an average life-span of less than a year and rarely more than two years. Extremes of longevity in shrews or mice are on the order of three to five years.

About the longevity or population dynamics of tropical bats we have at present little information.

Some years ago, when I was working briefly as a guest at the Gorgas Memorial Laboratory in Panama City, Dr. Harold Trapido told me of an accidental study of longevity in vampires. In 1935 or before, a colony of vampires had been established in the laboratory for use in an investigation of a vampire-transmitted disease of cattle. When the scientists engaged in these studies left Panama, the animal caretaker, receiving no order to the contrary, continued to maintain the bats. In about 1946, Dr. Trapido came to Panama and was assigned the administrative task of overseeing the animal quarters. He requested a census and was surprised to find listed a colony of vampires. On inquiry, these proved to include not only a few of the original bats (marked in some fashion), perhaps 11 years or so in captivity, but abundant descendants of these and of others long dead. We do not know how many generations had bred and were still represented. In nature, vampires may not survive as long because of a more challenging life.

Parasites and disease take their toll among bats, particularly among those that live in colonial aggregates. Many bat caves are inhabited by blood-sucking bugs (related to bed bugs). Almost all bats carry several other kinds of external parasites. The most common are modified flies. One family of such flies is flightless; rarely is more than one of these found on a single bat. Flies of another family of bat parasites are small and look something like fruit flies. A dozen or more per bat is not uncommon. A number of mites or chiggers also infest bats. In Mexico, a red mite feeds on the edge of the ear of the sheath-tailed bat, *Balantiopteryx*. At a distance a row of these mites gives the ears a look of being piped with red. Bats may also harbor fleas, lice, and ticks.

None of these parasites, which in some cases are restricted to a single species of bats, feed on men. Curiously, they disappear within a few days from bats kept in captivity.

A WHO'S WHO OF BATS

Bats make up the order Chiroptera, a name taken from the Greek and meaning "hand-wing." There are two suborders, Megachiroptera and Microchiroptera. The former has one family only, the latter has 17. All of these, with their most important subfamilies, genera and species are listed in the overleaf table.

The Megachiroptera are generally believed to be more primitive than the Microchiroptera but to have evolved with them from a common ancestor. That they are more primitive is supported by anatomical evidence. Their skeleton is less specialized; in other words, it is more like that of their ancestors. The shoulder girdle is less modified for flight, for example, and they have large, relatively typical mammalian eyes. Except for *Rousettus*, they do not echolocate. Dependence on vision may be taken to be a primitive feature in this group. Some systematists have concluded, therefore, that primitively bats were frugivorous. I cannot take issue with this. Certainly once bats

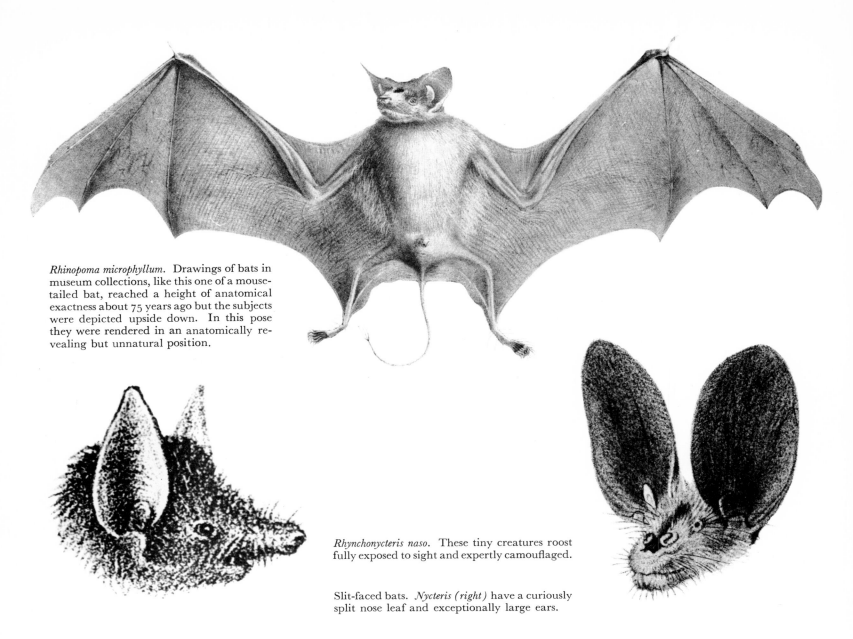

Rhinopoma microphyllum. Drawings of bats in museum collections, like this one of a mouse-tailed bat, reached a height of anatomical exactness about 75 years ago but the subjects were depicted upside down. In this pose they were rendered in an anatomically revealing but unnatural position.

Rhynchonycteris naso. These tiny creatures roost fully exposed to sight and expertly camouflaged.

Slit-faced bats. *Nycteris (right)* have a curiously split nose leaf and exceptionally large ears.

are aloft, hunting insects at night by vision would be impractical. Almost all bats *are* nocturnal and there is no reason to suppose that they were or could have been substantially otherwise in the past. Therefore, it seems reasonable to conclude that before sonar systems evolved they must have fed on fruit or flowers, the odor of which would have helped identify their positions.

On the other hand, the Megachiroptera and the Microchiroptera may have evolved independently from nonflying insectivorous and/or herbivorous or frugivorous ancestors. One line could have evolved flight without sonar and the other line flight with sonar. Otherwise one would expect or hope to find primitive Microchiroptera, either living or as fossils, which were frugivorous or which gave evidence of having been frugivorous by having quite differently formed teeth. The question cannot as yet be resolved on the basis of available evidence.

The single family making up the suborder Megachiroptera is the Pteropodidae or pteropodids—the flying foxes and their smaller relatives. Many of the pteropodids are very large, as the name of the suborder would suggest. (But the names may also be misleading: some of the micros are larger than some of the macros.) The largest, several species of the flying fox genus, *Pteropus,* have wing spreads of 4-5 feet (1.2-1.5 meters) and they may weigh 2 pounds (0.9 kilograms) or more. Their body, excluding the wings, is like that of a large pigeon. Many species, however, even some of the genus *Pteropus,* are substantially smaller. Bats of the abundant and widespread genera, *Rousettus* and *Cynopterus* for example, may have wing spreads of about 18-24 inches (0.45-0.6 meters) and weigh, perhaps, a half-pound (0.2 kilograms). There are also several extraordinarily small, flower-feeding genera such as *Macroglossus,* with wing spreads of about 10 inches (0.25 meters).

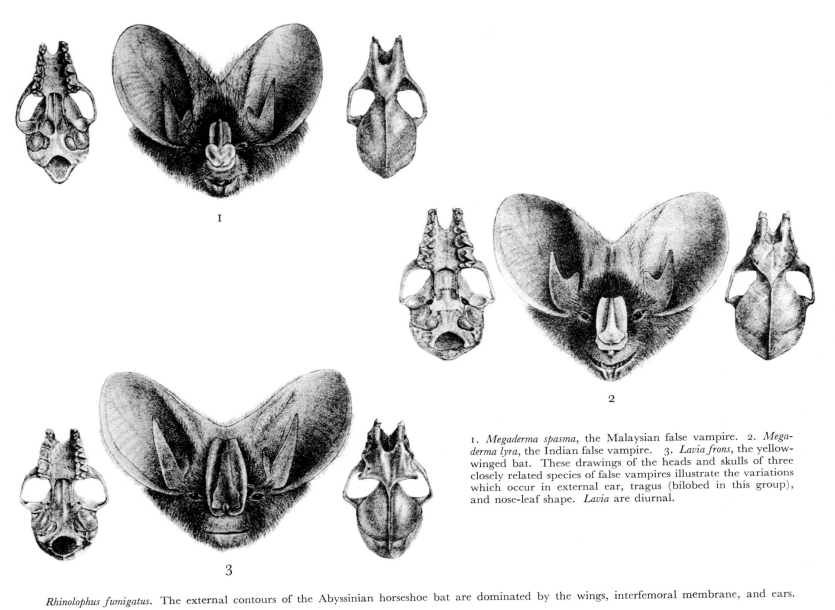

1. *Megaderma spasma*, the Malaysian false vampire. 2. *Megaderma lyra*, the Indian false vampire. 3. *Lavia frons*, the yellow-winged bat. These drawings of the heads and skulls of three closely related species of false vampires illustrate the variations which occur in external ear, tragus (bilobed in this group), and nose-leaf shape. *Lavia* are diurnal.

1

2

3

Rhinolophus fumigatus. The external contours of the Abyssinian horseshoe bat are dominated by the wings, interfemoral membrane, and ears.

Family	Range	Common Name	* Genera and species discussed and depicted in this book	Common Name	Range
			Suborder Megachiroptera		
Pteropodidae (pteropodids)	Old World tropics	Flying foxes and fruit bats	*Pteropus giganteus* *	Flying fox	India
			Rousettus aegyptiacus *	Dog-faced bat	Near East and Africa
			Cynopterus brachyotis *	Short-nosed fruit bat	South East Asia
			Epomophorus sp. *	Epaulette bat	Central Africa
			Lissonycteris angolensis	Long-haired fruit bat	Central Africa
			Eonycteris sp.	Dawn bat	Southeast Asia
			Hypsignathus monstrosus *	Hammer-headed bat	Central Africa
			Suborder Microchiroptera		
Rhinopomatidae (rhinopomatids)	Egypt, Near East, India and Indonesia	Mouse-tailed bats	*Rhinopoma microphyllum* *	Mouse-tailed bat	Egypt
Emballonuridae (emballonurids)	Worldwide tropics	Sheath-tailed bats	*Balantiopteryx plicata*	Sac-winged bat	Mexico and Central America
			Rynchonycteris naso	Sharp-nosed bat	Central and South America
			Saccopteryx bilineata	White-lined bat	Central America
Nycteridae (nycterids)	Central Africa and Indonesia	Slit-faced bats	*Nycteris* sp. *	Slit-faced bat	Central Africa and Indonesia
Megadermatidae (megadermatids)	Southeast Asia, Australia and Central Africa	False vampires	*Megaderma spasma* *	Maleysian false vampire	Southeast Asia
			Megaderma lyra *	Indian false vampire	Southeast Asia
			Lavia frons *	Yellow-winged bat	Central Africa
Hipposideridae (hipposiderids)	Old World tropics	Leaf-nosed bats	*Hipposideros commersoni gigas* *	Giant African leaf-nosed bat	West Africa
			Hipposideros lankadiva	Ceylon leaf-nosed bat	Ceylon
Rhinolophidae (rhinolophids)	Old World, temperate and tropical	Horseshoe bats	*Rhinolophus subrufus*	Philippine horseshoe bat	Philippines
			Rhinolophus fumigatus *	Abyssinian horseshoe bat	North and Central Africa
Noctilionidae (noctilionids)	Neotropical	Bulldog bats	*Noctilio leporinus* *	Fishing bulldog bat	Central and South America
			Noctilio labialis	Lesser bulldog bat	Central and South America
Phyllostomatidae (phyllostomatids)	Neotropical, Southwestern U.S.A.	Spear-nosed bats			
Subfamily Chilonycterinae	Central and South America	Mustache bats	*Chilonycteris parnellii* *	Greater mustache bat	Mexico, Central America and the Caribbean
			Chilonycteris psilotis	Lesser mustache bat	Mexico and Central America
			Pteronotus sp.	Naked-backed bats	Central and South America
			Mormoops sp.	Leaf-chinned bats	Central and South America

The Megachiroptera feed on fruit and flowers. The frugivorous genera exploit a variety of wild fruits and berries. When abundant in the vicinity of banana or fig orchards, they may be pests. However, bananas which are being raised for market are usually picked while green, apparently before they are attractive to bats. A regimen of fruit or flowers, of course, restricts these bats to a tropical or subtropical distribution since the flowering and fruit-ripening seasons in temperate climates are too brief to support them year-round. None of the Megachiroptera is known to prey on animals except for insects which they ingest inadvertently along with fruit or flowers.

The Megachiroptera are found only in the Old World. They range from outlying Pacific islands to Australia, through Southeast Asia, the Near East and almost all of Africa. The individual genera, however, have more limited distributions, some of which are quite interesting. The flying foxes, *Pteropus*, extend throughout the range of the suborder excepting only Africa, where there are none.

Family	Range	Common Name	* Genera and species discussed and depicted in this book	Common Name	Range
			Suborder Microchiroptera		
Phyllostomatinae	Neotropical		Macrotus waterhousii * . . .	Big-eared bat	Mexico and Central America
			Vampyrum spectrum *	False vampire	The Caribbean and Southwest U.S.A.
			Phyllostomus hastatus	Spear-nosed bat	Central and South America Central and South America
Carolliinae	Neotropical		Carollia perspicillata	Short-tailed bat	Central and South America
Glossophaginae . .	Neotropical into Southwestern U.S.A.	Long-tongued bats or nectar-feeding bats	Glossophaga sp.	Long-tongued bats	Mexico, Central and South America
			Monophyllus redmani * . . .	Jamaican long-tongued bat	Jamaica
			Leptonycteris sanborni * . . .	or long-nosed bat. . . .	Mexico and Southwest U.S.A.
Stenoderminae . .	Neotropical		Artibeus jamaicensis *	Jamaican fruit bat	Neotropics
			Artibeus nanus *	Dwarf fruit bat	Mexico and Central America
			Uroderma bilobatum	Tent-making bat	Central and South America
Phyllonycterinae . .	The Carribean . . .	Flower bats	Erophylla sezekorni	Brown flower bat	The Caribbean
			Phyllonycteris aphylla * . . .	Jamaican flower bat . . .	Jamaica
Desmodontidae . . . (desmodontids)	Neotropical	Vampires	Desmodus rotundus murinus * .	Vampire	Mexico, Central and South America
Natalidae . . . . . (natalids)	Neotropical	Funnel-eared bats . .	Natalus sp.	Funnel-eared bat	Mexico, Central and South America
			Chilonatalus micropus	Jamaican long-legged bat	Jamaica
Vespertilionidae . . . (vespertilionids)	Worldwide	Common bats	Myotis lucifugus	Little brown bat	U.S. and Canada
			Pisonyx vivesi	Fishing bat	Baja California
			Pipistrellus sp.	Pipistrelle	Worldwide
			Eptesicus fuscus	Big brown bat	North America
			Lasiurus cinereus *	Hoary bat	North America
			Lasiurus borealis	Red bat	North America
			Euderma maculatum * . . .	Spotted bat	Western U.S.
			Plecotus townsendii *	Big-eared bat	U.S, Canada and Mexico
			Antrozous pallidus *	Long-eared bat, pallid bat	Western U.S. and Mexico
Molossidae . . . . . (molossids)	Worldwide	Free-tailed bats . . .	Tadarida brasiliensis . . . . mexicana *	Mexican free-tailed bat; guano bat	Southern U.S. and Mexico
			Tadarida molossa *	Big free-tailed bat	Southwestern U.S., Mexico and Central America
			Molossus rufus nigricans * . .	Black mastiff bat, velvet bat	Mexico and Central America
			Cheiromeles torquata	Naked free-tailed bat . . .	Malaysia

Why have flying foxes successfully colonized Madagascar and the Comoro Islands and yet not reached the African mainland? We do not know. Perhaps they cannot compete with other African bats or other frugivorous organisms; perhaps they are exceptionally vulnerable to some African tree-climbing carnivores. The predominance of flying foxes as part of island faunas (where there are few or no carnivorous enemies) suggests that they may have evolved away from some protective devices on which continental forms depend for survival.

The genus Rousettus, the dog-faced bats, are rarely found on islands. Uniquely among the Megachiroptera, Rousettus have evolved a sonar system for orientation in flight, emitting sounds and listening to and analyzing the echoes which return. This may account in part for Rousettus' extraordinary distribution. With their sonar, Rousettus have been able to exploit dark caves as roosts, thereby sheltering themselves from predators and from weather. The absence of caves or the difficulty of finding them on demand in new territory may restrict their invasion of islands. On the mainland, new caves may be discovered and colonized at leisure, over tens of thousands of years. If a few *Rousettus* were to reach a new island, carried by a storm, say, they would be unlikely to chance upon a completely unknown cave entrance that they could shelter in before they had succumbed to enemies or to old age.

Excepting only four genera, the Megachiroptera roost in trees in full view. In some cases they are too large to enter caves, crevices, or hollow trees. Basically, however, their restriction to external roosts must be associated with their lack of echolocation. They cannot orient in total darkness. Furthermore, most of them cannot walk except by crawling along branches upside down. Thus it is difficult for them to enter enclosed spaces on wing or on foot.

Eonycteris (very similar in appearance but only distantly allied to *Rousettus*), live in the same caves as *Rousettus* but orient visually. How can they fly in a dark cave? My best bet is that they occupy only those caves which are partly lighted at dawn and dusk—straight caves with large entrances pointing roughly east or west, for example. No one has yet investigated the matter.

The cave-dwelling genera are among the few pteropodids which are drab in appearance. They come in various shades of brown. In the dark, colors or markings cannot serve either as species or as sex-recognition signals or for camouflage against potential predators. Almost all of the other Megachiroptera are brightly colored, often with shades of red, auburn, gold, or yellow, or marked with spots or even stripes.

Outdoor roosting and a diet of fruit—abundant and easily procured in the tropics—probably favor large size. A large bat has fewer temperature-regulating problems because its mass is large relative to its surface. These considerations may account for the generally large size of the Megachiroptera. Many of the more exclusively flower-feeding genera are small. Smallness may be favored by the mechanics of hovering.

The most primitive Microchiroptera

The most primitive living family of Microchiroptera are the mouse-tailed bats, the Rhinopomatidae, which now have a relict distribution. They can be presumed to have been passed by evolutionarily and to have competed poorly in nature except under special or local conditions. In Egypt they often roost in tombs or monuments, as do *Rousettus*, and are therefore sometimes called tomb bats.

A closely related family, the sheath-tailed bats or Emballonuridae, roost in external or semi-external locations, favoring tree trunks (often palms), church belfries or other open or well-lighted parts of buildings (even abandoned air-raid shelters), cliff faces, shallow, lighted caves, and the undersides of bridges. They almost invariably roost on vertical surfaces, hanging by their toes with their wrists propped against the surface and their back facing outward. They can run swiftly up or down these surfaces, which are usually rough and offer many toeholds. Their preference for open roosts may represent some limitation on their ability to orient in total darkness but other unknown physiological adaptations may also be concerned.

Their roosts are sometimes hot or even sun-baked, sometimes deeply shady. Some genera roost in low-humidity sites—an isolated palm tree in a dry courtyard, for example—while others are found only on the lower side of tree trunks overhanging water or in equivalent sites. Many emballonurids roost close to the ground among the damp buttresses of giant trees in the tropical rain forest. Those species in shallow caves or belfries form colonies numbering in the thousands. Many other species, however, live in groups of several dozen or less and some species are probably solitary.

Emballonurids often have marked or mottled fur, apparently for camouflage. In *Saccopteryx bilineata*, for example, the back is black except for two white stripes in the shape of an hour-glass. When they roost in dense shade, under the jungle canopy, their markings break up their contours. Their roosting posture also is confusing to the eye. I say this empirically, having been unable to identify them several times though they were in full view. Many of the sheath-tailed bats roost in small colonies, up to several dozen, but seem to arrange themselves in a spaced-out fashion. The irregular pattern created by the group tends to mimic natural irregularities, that of bark, for example.

On one occasion I was seeking a colony of *Rhynchonycteris* (which are very small and have a mottled black, white, orange, yellow, and brown pelage) that was known to roost on the underside of a particular bridge in Panama. After two of us had searched under the small bridge earnestly but fruitlessly for some time, I decided to throw some rocks at the girders in a final attempt to scare the bats out of possible hiding places. No sooner had I thrown the first rock than the "rivets" in the girders flew away. Perhaps 30 *Rhynchonycteris* had been roosting, fully exposed, on the sides of the girders; with their dark, rusty color, their spaced-out assemblage, and their small size and roundish shape, they effectively mimicked the rivets. A few weeks later I encountered what I took to be a small group of tree frogs on the trunk of a large tree on Barro Colorada Island. As I approached, one of the frogs hopped away; the other three *flew* away. They proved to be *Saccopteryx*.

The sheath-tailed bats have an endearing characteristic from the point of view of a physiologist who works only with living subjects. By and large, they cannot be induced to bite. They seem to lack entirely the behavioral pattern of biting in defense. I presume their best defense in nature to be camouflage or, if necessary, rapid flight. But why would this be true of emballonurids and not of other bats? Roosting as they do, outdoors and in the tropics, their body temperature, even if it drops while they are at rest, as is the case for some bats, would be quite high. Thus their neuro-muscular system would be in an alert state, ready to respond rapidly. For such small, alert animals, escape if practical would almost surely be more effective than the trivial deterrent-effect their bite would have.

The Nycteridae, or slit-faced bats, are another apparently relict group. The family's common name refers to the shape of the nose leaf, a fleshy appendage around and above the nostrils which occurs in several families of bats and is believed to function as part of their sonar orientation system. In the Nycteridae, the nose leaf is split along the midline, giving the face a cleaved appearance.

The slit-faced bats usually roost in hollow trees, in small, enclosed, and undisturbed buildings (cellars, empty water towers, unoccupied huts), in culverts, and in aardvark and porcupine burrows. They are also found roosting in the branches of trees but usually in the jungle canopies, well hidden and shaded by dense foliage. They roost in small colonies, from a few to as many as a dozen or two. They dehydrate very easily; their roosts seem to be chosen for high humidity. In captivity, the slit-faced bats do not appear to grasp the concept of drinking from a dish though almost all other bats do so without training. Perhaps in nature they drink droplets of water from foliage or even catch raindrops in flight.

The slit-faced bats hunt insects, spiders, and scorpions that are resting on surfaces of rocks, walls, tree trunks, or foliage. These bats have a hovering flight when hunting and search slowly and systematically up and down along their route, often flying only a few inches from the object they are scanning. They may enter homes in such hunting flights. In the Congo, for example, I was able to capture individuals of two species of *Nycteris* by lying awake near an open bedroom window until I could hear a bat flying in my room. I would then close the window and allow the bat to rid the house of its insect population before cap-turing it. I attempted to convert one such bat into a dynamic insecticide by screening the windows and doors after it had entered but not otherwise disturbing or con-fining it. I filled many conspicuous and accessible recep-tacles with drinking water as well, but to no avail. The bat rid the house of insects, and died of dehydration about three days later.

Closely related to the Nycteridae are the Megader-matidae or false vampires. Colonies usually number several to several dozen individuals which roost well spaced out.

Some roost in caves or border heaps, others in open roomy attics or similar sites; but they are also found roosting fully exposed to sunlight and weather on the branches of acacia trees in the savannah.

The meaning of "Peep, peep"

The relatively large Asiatic *Megaderma lyra* is carnivorous, feeding on birds, lizards, tree frogs, small bats, and other small mammals as well as large insects. The other false vampires are principally insectivorous or partly carniv-orous. They hunt along walls, tree trunks, and vegetation like the nycterids, moving slowly and deliberately up and down with a hovering sort of flight. *Lavia*, the African genus, have been reported to fly and to pursue and capture insects in broad daylight.

I was fortunate to have several examples of *Megaderma lyra* in captivity for some time in Ceylon. I found two of the females to be carrying young which had been totally concealed by their mother's wing. The mothers, after having adapted to cage life, would often leave the infants hanging from the ceiling while they themselves preened, foraged, or slept. I wondered at first how the infants gained immunity from attack by predaceous relatives since they are of edible size and obviously vulnerable. The infants apparently identify themselves vocally whenever they are disturbed. If I jarred the cage, for example, or if a bat landed on it, or if the babies heard another bat approaching, they would invariably emit a "peep, peep" which I believe carried the message: "I too am a false vampire. Do not eat me." Since few if any other predators would have access to these vulnerable young on cave or attic ceilings it was probably quite safe for them to express themselves out loud.

Several genera of the Hipposideridae or leaf-nosed bats are recognized. One, *Hipposideros*, is almost universal within the family range. Colonial aggregates in some species, the giant Ceylonese *H. lankadiva*, for example, may number thousands while other species form groups of less than a dozen. One small African species roosts only in fallen, hollow trees or in the ecological equivalent—damp and dark culverts. Three or four species of *Hipposideros* are often found inhabiting much the same terrain. Almost all of the hipposiderids roost in dark and humid caves or their equivalent but a few species roost optionally out-of-doors in jungle trees or boulder heaps. A colony of some hundreds of *Hipposideros* even moves into the spacious and airy attic of the stately Mount Lavinia Hotel in Ceylon as the rainy season starts and brings with it 100 per cent relative humidity and almost constant overcast. The smaller hipposiderids, on the whole, roost in groups with the individuals well spaced out. They do not walk or even seem to shift their ceiling-hold and so must be free to land and take off without encumberance. Their spacing seems to allow for free individual movement.

When I first encountered *H. lankadiva*, I also discovered how vulnerable bats can be to diurnal predators. I was searching for these leaf-nosed bats in a cave in Ceylon and was accompanied by a vacationing American couple who reacted as do most lay enthusiasts—by waiting for me outside the cave entrance. Inside I found thousands of *H. lankadiva*. In capturing a sample of the population I frightened some ten or twelve bats enough to make them fly out of the cave into full daylight. My friends watched with awe as these bats were individually spotted by jungle crows, which approached from above and behind, forced them down, overpowered and devoured them. I saw the last two strays being finished off myself. It was a dramatic demonstration of how poorly adapted these leaf-nosed bats are for diurnal emergence. None survived more than 20 minutes, and without casualty or difficulty to the crows.

The caves at Monte Alban have been an important source of a number of hipposiderid species, as well as other bats, some of them discovered there for the first time. Ever since naturalists first visited the Philippines, these caves have been considered an obligatory part of their itinerary. In 1955, I went to the Philippines specifically to study, *in situ*, as many living species of bats as I could. As I approached Luzon by plane, I engaged several young naval officers who were fellow passengers in conversation about some of the classical collecting sites. All but Monte Alban were believed to be accessible but I was informed, among others by a lieutenant in Naval Intelligence, that the caves at Monte Alban were a major hideout and stronghold of the Huks (Communist-oriented insurrectionists). They said I would not only be forbidden to go to Monte Alban by the American authorities but would also be excluded from the caves by the Huks, killed for my money and equipment, or kidnapped for ransom. Their view was confirmed and reinforced by countless officers at my base of operations near Manila.

Accordingly, being young, impulsive, and driven to succeed, I went to Monte Alban the next week to see for myself rather than forego the abundance of bats known to roost there. I found it to be a region of great natural beauty—a low, round, verdant hill pock-marked with cave entrances and approached by a picturesque meadow. By the side of the hill flowed a lovely stream which tumbled in the distance down a small but engaging waterfall from a sapphire blue lake beyond. In the far distance, I could see bamboo rafts, loaded with firewood, being guided down the lake by single boatmen while along the stream trotted a number of rather primitive-looking young men carrying bundles of firewood and kindling. In the peaceful meadow was a movie company on location filming an adventure story. The wives and children of the staff and actors were cavorting and picnicking in the background.

Huks they may have been. Indeed, the six or eight young men who gathered around me in friendly curiosity and spent the day guiding me to and through the caves, netting bats and lizards with me, and carrying most of my heavy cages, may well have been Huks, too. I sought no political identification from them. We didn't discuss politics or world affairs. I was to return several times—apparently the only American other than my driver to do so in those days—and had only the warmest of casual, friendly relationships with them. I felt rewarded both zoologically and as a human being.

The Rhinolophidae or horseshoe bats are closely related to the hipposiderids. They take their name from the shape of the lower portion of their nose leaf. Some of the horseshoe bats have solved the physiological problems of survival in a temperate winter characterized by cold and scarcity of food. All of the species so far studied feed on flying insects which are, of course, rare in winter. (Insects usually over-winter in a state of suspended metabolism called diapause.) Several species of horseshoe bats, particularly *Rhinolophus ferrum-equinum* and *R. hipposideros* of Europe, are known to hibernate. This involves fat storage in the fall, suspension of temperature regulation, and other adaptations.

In the tropics, *Rhinolophus* vary from tiny to exceptionally-large forms roosting principally in dark caves or hollow trees. Several species, normally brownish, have bright-red or auburn variants; their colors are thought to be fortuitous or diet-related since these species have no occasion to see or appreciate such coloring.

I have been surprised at how frequently I have found rhinolophids roosting adjacent to running streams or rivulets or, in fact, often literally behind waterfalls. Whether they require high humidity or gain some other advantage from these roosts has not been established.

Many of the rhinolophids adapt well to captivity, learn quickly, and are exceptionally responsive. When I had *Rhinolophus subrufus* in my temporary laboratory in the Philippines, I was visited one day by a first-grade teacher and some of her charges, all children of U.S. service families. About 15 of the children returned the next day to volunteer their assistance in caring for my bats. Realistically uncertain of the reliability of six year olds, I assigned them the task of delivering a daily collection of large live insects with which to feed the bats. After they had served devotedly for a week, I taught them how to clean the cages, refresh the water supply, and eventually to feed the bats.

The most time-consuming bats at that time were a small group of the very attractive *Rhinolophus subrufus* which had to be handfed. They had quickly learned to associate my hand with being fed, however, and would swarm over as soon as I reached into the cage and bite my fingers. The bites carried no connotation of hostility, only good appetite and poor discrimination. Bat bites, however, are painful even though they do little damage. For this reason, and lacking child-size gloves, I forebore allowing any of the children to feed the *Rhinolophus*.

"Silly bat"

After a couple of weeks, one particularly gentle child begged to be allowed to feed them and I yielded. Everything seemed to go well and I returned to my experiments. When I checked back later, I saw my helper with a *R. subrufus* hanging determinedly by its teeth from her index finger. Visions of an irate mother descending on me with angry cries of "Monster!" raced through my mind. But as I approached I realized the child was laughing and announcing calmly and proudly to her friends through chuckles, "Look, he's biting me! Silly bat." And indeed they are silly at times but very engaging.

The Noctilionidae, or bulldog bats, consist of a single Neotropical genus, *Noctilio*. Unlike the families already described, the bulldog bats walk well. This permits them to exploit a variety of roosts.

I once placed a group of lesser bulldog bats in a borrowed mouse cage in Panama. The next day I was chagrined to find them all missing. After mentally accusing everyone of sabotaging my experiments, I returned with the same cage to capture more bats in the same hot and guano-dusty church attic. This time, as I placed the bats in the cage through the door, I saw them crawl freely out again through a small hole. The cage, built of quarter-inch hardware cloth, was missing a single strand of wire for a length of three squares. The all but invisible defect was to these bats a grand portal to freedom. This was the first of my many experiences with the impressive escape capacity of bats that can walk or crawl.

The greater bulldog bat, *Noctilio leporinus*, hunts flying insects but also fishes in fresh or salt water. These bats differ from their smaller relatives in having greatly enlarged hind feet and claws with which they gaff the fish. They roost in small colonies in hollow trees and in rocky niches.

The Phyllostomatidae or spear-nosed bats fill a large number of ecological niches in the New World equivalent to those of many of the Old World families listed above. The primitive subfamily, the Chilonycterinae or mustache bats, are quite distinct and may someday be given family status. They lack a nose leaf but are adorned instead with elaborate lips and lip leaves which are held, when sonar signals are being emitted, in a megaphone shape, perhaps to serve as a sound-beaming device.

The genera *Chilonycteris* and *Pteronotus* adapt well to captivity, especially because of their ability to walk, and have proved to be major figures in our studies of echolocation. On the other hand, we have not yet succeeded in bringing even one individual of another genus, *Mormoops*, to the laboratory in good condition. They are among the most beautiful of bats, with a rich pelage, countersunk ears, and a most engaging general aspect. All of the Chilonycterinae occur in a variety of colors—grey, tan, brown, canary yellow, orange, and auburn as well as some mixtures of these. The color may be genetic, dietary, or even seasonal. We do not know. We have observed, however, that the beautifully colored red and orange individuals, whatever the species they may belong to, inexplicably do not adapt well to captivity.

Chilonycteris and *Pteronotus* seem to require heat and humidity. These bats will relax only if they are allowed to roost in tightly clumped groups. Natural colonies of *Chilonycteris*, *Pteronotus*, and *Mormoops* often number tens of thousands. At times the three genera intermingle, while at other times they roost quite separately.

The next most anatomically generalized of the spear-nosed bats are those of the subfamily Phyllostomatinae. Some are insectivorous, others carnivorous, frugivorous, or omnivorous. They all have elaborate and often very large nose leaves and most have exceptionally large ears as well. Their appearance is often dominated by these appendages. The largest American bat, the carnivorous *Vampyrum spectrum*, with a wing spread of up to about 30 inches (75 centimeters) belongs to this group, as does the insectivorous genus *Macrotus*. Some of these genera live in small groups of up to a dozen or two but some, and *Macrotus* is an example, often form colonies of several hundred individuals or more. None walks well. They roost in caves, hollow trees, boulder heaps, culverts, and under bridges.

In captivity, *Macrotus* do very well and rapidly learn to self-feed from a dish, provided that they are not tightly confined. On collecting trips in Jamaica, I have often had to allow captive *Macrotus* the freedom of my hotel bathroom in order to ensure their survival. Since I invariably have to spare the nerves of the chambermaids as well as the other guests, I usually cage and release these bats several times a day according to a tight schedule. In one hotel in Montego Bay, I was especially pleased by the high-ceilinged bathroom in which our dozen *Macrotus* were able to roost comfortably from a molding. On the third or fourth day of our stay, however, I was shocked to notice that an inconspicuous window high in the bathroom wall opened onto the main hallway. Whenever anyone chanced to look up through the window, as had certainly happened repeatedly, the row of bats could be seen, spaced out, napping and preening, and occasionally eating.

Modifying the environment

Several advanced subfamilies of spear-nosed bats are exclusively frugivorous or almost so. Among the Stenoderminae such as *Artibeus*, white or cream-colored facial stripes are common. These bats often roost on the underside of palm leaves, under eaves or bridges, or in culverts. The stripes may well help conceal them from predators looking up from below. In Summit Gardens in Panama, a specimen palm at the side of the driveway provides a home for several dozen stripe-faced *Uroderma* which along with a small species of *Artibeus* are the only bats which substantially modify their environment for roosting purposes. They bite across the middle of large palm leaves, leaving a row of tooth holes looking like hemstitching. The leaf then folds down like a tent and the bats, hanging underneath at the apex, gain shelter and protection from predators. Their roost is revealed by the dense growth of seedlings below, which sprout from seeds that they have discarded.

Carollia, a small, almost ubiquitous tropical species, form dense cave colonies of several thousands. Once I encountered them in a rarely visited cave near Penonemé in Panama where not only did strong local taboos exclude intruders but, in addition, the chamber which the bats occupied was accessible only by a small entrance in a vertical cliff face. The upper walls and the ceiling were lined with tight clusters of *Carollia* totally indifferent to me and even to my light! I was able to pluck these bats from the ceiling by hand. I can only guess that these fully alert bats had inhabited this isolated cave long enough to have modified their escape behavior. Another chamber of the same cave, but an accessible one, was densely inhabited by mustache bats. The ceiling and the walls were fur-lined almost to the floor. In order to capture some as they flew, I simply held an insect net aloft and lowered it as it filled with three different species.

A few genera of glossophagine bats, a subfamily of spear-nosed bats—*Leptonycteris*, for example—form large colonies. I have seen a group numbering over 100,000 in a cave in southern Mexico. In Jamaica, bats of the Caribbean genus *Monophyllus* occur by the tens of thousands in several well known caves. Other genera form small colonies of up to a few dozen at most and may also roost solitarily. *Glossophaga*, tiny and beautifully proportioned, are fierce and unbending. *Lonchophylla* feed happily while being handheld even

when newly captured. Their charm as they lap sugarwater from a medicine dropper, inserting their incredible tongue through the terminal hole, defies description.

The Phyllonycterinae or flower bats, not closely allied to the previous group, are exceptional in beauty and grace. In spite of their name, the feeding habits of these bats are not actually established. The Jamaican flower bat, thought to be extinct until recently, has very short but dense, creamy-beige fur resembling mohair cloth or plush. We found these bats to be uncommon but certainly not extinct. With a good light, in St. Clair Cave, one can pinpoint them among thousands of other bats on the cave ceiling by their pallid pelage. The proportions of their long flexible legs and long upper arms distinguish them from any other bats known to me but I have no evidence which bears on the significance or utility of these proportions.

Legendary namesakes

The Desmodontidae or vampires are closely related to the spear-nosed bats and apparently derived from them. Three genera of vampires are known, all of them Neotropical. No vampire bats have ever existed in the Old World. The legends of vampires in European folklore all concerned nocturnal, manlike spirits which rose from the dead to feed on human blood. When early European naturalists discovered blood-feeding bats—nocturnal, secretive, and winged—they named them vampires in honor of those legendary beings. Thus the bats acquired the evil reputation of their namesakes. In actual fact vampire bats are small (1 ounce or 30 grams), timid, and rather inoffensive.

My first face-to-face encounter with vampires took place in a tidal cave in Panama. Vampires are among the most common mammals in Panama and one substantial but inaccessible colony used to inhabit a culvert in front of a luxury hotel in Panama City. On the occasion of my visiting the tidal cave, I was rushed by the timing of the tides which allowed me only a short time to enter, find and capture the bats, and return to higher land but I was also handicapped by naïveté and an unavoidable leeriness. I entered the cave—a long, narrow corridor with a rising floor that converged with the ceiling in the distance. The interior end consisted of an intricate series of crevices in the boulders. I soon spotted a small colony (about 20 individuals) of vampires but, moving over-cautiously, I allowed them to retreat into the interior crevices before I could net them.

Crawling to the apex of the cave, I was able to grasp one vampire's wing as it clung to the interior of a crevice. I tugged gently; the vampire tugged back. We had reached an impasse until the vampire, reaching for a more secure hold, momentarily released its grip and I was able to start to pull it from the crevice. The bat responded by swinging around, screeching violently, and trying to take flight. I was unnerved by the activity and let go. The bat then ran up my arm to freedom; I leapt back and up, struck my head solidly against the stone ceiling, and collapsed half conscious to the floor.

As I did so, I noticed that the floor was soft and that I seemed at the same time to be enveloped by a nauseating odor. Looking down, I discovered myself cushioned by a very large and very dead boa constricter which had apparently been washed in by the tide. Much later, I was able to go on to capture two vampires which subsequently lived long and productive lives at Harvard.

Vampires usually live in colonies of several dozen to several hundred and, not surprisingly, favor roosts near herds of domestic animals on which they feed. They take well to captivity, become docile and cooperative, and feed on refrigerated blood. In fact the only problem involved in maintaining vampires in captivity is that someone must be willing to be the butt of endless jokes when he goes to the slaughterhouse each week to pick up the blood.

The Natalidae, or funnel-eared bats are nowhere really common. Only one genus, *Natalus*, is recognized. They roost in dark caves and favor segregated niches, away from other bats. Their aggregates may number several hundred and consist of well spaced-out individuals. We know little of these small, long-legged bats with very attractive, platypus-like faces. They eat readily in captivity but nevertheless survive poorly.

Shirt-collar hideaway

In St. Claire Cave in Jamaica, there are sizable populations not only of *Natalus* but of a miniature relative belonging to the subgenus, *Chilonatalus*. *Chilonatalus* are among the smallest bats and the smallest mammals known and are exceptionally attractive. Daring not hope that we could keep them alive, we nevertheless took two individuals back to our hotel in Ocho Rios. At the hotel, the bats proved willing to eat. To encourage them to eat enough to support their high metabolism we would open all the doors and windows for several hours each day, thus allowing wild insects to enter, and then close the room and allow *Chilonatalus* to hunt and feed as if in nature. They did this effectively, apparently not being inhibited by the confinement of walls.

After several days, one of our *Chilonatalus* disappeared. In spite of a meticulous search, we were unable to find it and gave it up for lost. The next day, after feeding, our

second *Chilonatalus* also disappeared. We were unwilling to give up this time. We turned the room inside out, searched under the beds, in the bedding and springs, under the mattresses, behind the furniture, in the bookshelves, and in every other possible hiding place. Finally, we narrowed our search to the clothes closet and, after another half hour, turned our pet out from a quiet rest under the button-down collar of my shirt. On subsequent days it again bedded down in the closet, where we kept all of the bats when we were out so as not to distress the chambermaid or the manager. It chose a challenging variety of roosts—inside the inner breast pocket of a jacket, in a trouser leg, in a shirt sleeve, or among the folds of laundered clothing.

The charm of our *Chilonatalus* and our devotion to her cannot be exaggerated. We fashioned a private cage for her trip to Yale out of a perforated, hard, cigarette-package fitted with a net perch and cotton-cushioned walls. She boarded the plane, well camouflaged as a pack of cigarettes, in my young associate's pocket. The other bats traveled much less surreptitiously in the cargo compartment or in specially fitted sample cases which we carried as hand baggage. Unfortunately, our favorite companion never reached Yale. En route to New Haven, our station wagon went over an exceptionally deep pothole and the jolt knocked *Chilonatalus* from her roost. The fall, short though it was to the bottom of the cigarette box, killed her.

The Vespertilionidae are the "common" bats of the world. Three exceptionally successful genera, *Myotis*, *Eptesicus*, and *Pipistrellus* have worldwide distributions. Almost all of the vespertilionids feed on flying insects. Many of them occupy buildings during the summer months in temperate climates and caves in the winter. Among their favorite roosts in the United States are attics and barns (especially for nursery colonies) or under shingles or behind shutters. Some species aggregate in large numbers, even tens of thousands, in winter cave-colonies or in tropical caves. Others are solitary or almost so.

In the Congo, I was quite surprised to find as many as five species of small vespertilionids roosting in the "thatched" roofs of native huts, in among the twigs. They are also reported to roost in the similar structure of birds' nests. Almost every well built but old tropical building of stature—churches, schoolhouses, and police stations—houses some vespertilionids, especially the genus *Scotophilus* in the Old World.

Not all vespertilionids hunt or feed alike. *Myotis macrotarsus*, an oriental species, and *Pisonyx*, of Baja California, both fish. Pallid bats, *Antrozous*, of the western United States, and the long-eared bats, *Plecotus*, hover along the ground and around vegetation, where they attempt to find terrestrial insects and other arthropods.

The "lit-lit" bat

The tiny Indonesian and Philippine bamboo bats, *Tylonycteris pachypus*, roost in the hollow core of growing bamboo. My first encounter with them was by remarkable good fortune. One day I was sitting by a fire in the jungle in Luzon with a group of Negritos who were helping me collect bats. We were speaking anecdotally of bats when one of the men, using the term "lit-lit," alluded to a bat which lived in bamboo shoots. I recalled having seen references to bamboo bats but not in the Philippines and, on his offering to show me such bats, expressed a high level of enthusiasm. Unfortunately my benefactor leapt up and ran off into the jungle before I could follow but I was given to understand that he located them by going along a jungle path and striking sharply at likely-looking bamboo shoots with the dull side of his machete. He would then listen for the disturbed squawks that these bats emit. He reappeared a few minutes later carrying a segment of green bamboo (about 5 centimeters in diameter) which he had severed above and below the natural segmental partitions. A large banana leaf was wrapped around the segment and tied with a vine. He announced that there were bats within and, indeed, when I gently shook the container I could hear squawks and scrambling within. I waited until I was back in my laboratory before undoing the binding and examining the bats. I then found some 20 *Tylonycteris* and two very rare tree frogs living together. The entrance to their roost consisted of a long crack which had apparently formed when the bamboo shoot was blown by a strong wind.

The Negritos are particularly familiar with this little bat because they use green bamboo segments as canteens, purses, storage containers, canisters, and even as cooking pots. A segment of bamboo, cut so as to preserve only a bottom partition, can be filled with meat, rice, and water, for example, the top stuffed with a folded palm leaf, and the entire piece placed directly in a fire. The contents cook long before the bamboo chars.

Lasiurus, the red and hoary bats, roost in trees in the forests of the United States and Canada in the summer. They migrate to the southern states for the winter. We know little of the physiology or behavior of their migrations.

Some years ago I assisted Dr. Griffin as he attempted to study red bats migrating over Cape Cod in the fall. On one occasion, I was to help him record the orientation pulses of these bats as they paused to feed on beetles over a miniature golf course in Falmouth. We chose this particular site because it provided a source of electricity for our recording equipment, was well lighted at night, permitting us to watch the bats that we were recording, and was but a short drive from the Griffins' summer home. The proprietor of the golf course made us promise not to reveal our mission lest his customers take their business elsewhere. So there we stood for several nights, our microphones fitted with great parabolic horns (designed to concentrate the sounds of distant bats), peering and pointing into the dark sky. One very irate man accused us of eavesdropping on his conversation with his wife. Several times we were accused of being Russian spies. Most of the verbally expressive people, however, concluded that we were students of flying saucers. One teenager who held to the flying saucer theory was accompanied by a friend who looked us over for a moment. The friend thereupon pronounced loudly and confidently, "Naw, they're listening to bats!"

No one believed *his* outlandish hypothesis.

The enormous success of the vespertilionids must be based in part on their ability to turn down their thermostat when at rest, thereby conserving energy. That is, several species are known to drop their body temperature, when at rest, to that of the environment. Such a drop, of course, requires changes in behavior and physiology to provide for security from enemies or from bad weather during the diurnal repose. Among other things, these bats exploit crevices or other highly secluded roosts (facilitated by very good crawling locomotion), have specialized sensory systems which serve to alert them to danger, and have developed brown fat as a heat-generating tissue associated with efficient arousal. In addition, dormant bats react fiercely to intruders, baring their teeth and emitting unpleasantly loud, high-pitched screeches.

In the winter, the temperate vespertilionids (excepting the migratory genera referred to above) hibernate in caves. They must not only choose reliable caves but reliably humid and warm individual roosts as well. They often form very large and densely clustered assemblages which presumably conserve heat by the approximation of bodies. Some species also cluster heavily in spring or summer nursery colonies where their combined body heat and the heat of decomposition of their guano on the floor may substantially raise the temperature of the chamber.

The molossids or free-tailed bats are all heavy-set, even when small, with bulky bodies and very long, narrow wings. They walk, scurry, and scuttle skillfully and during the day, even when pursued, often do so in preference to taking flight. The molossids often form truly enormous colonies like the nursery colonies in Texas mentioned above. Some few species such as the giant *Cheiromeles*, the naked free-tailed bat of Malaysia, inhabit hollow trees; they may be too large to enter or fly in caves. Some molossids roosts in cliff faces or in crevices in boulders. Many choose intensely hot roosts. But by far the bulk of molossids roosts in buildings. Almost any suitably built building in the tropics houses a colony of several hundred to several thousand molossids. Old school houses, churches, barracks, police stations, court houses, and city halls are choice locations. I have learned to look for wooden ceilings, tile roofs, and wooden casements as the most promising signs. The bats live under the tiles or in the roof space above the ceiling or in the hollow casements or walls. Their presence, if not revealed by the smell of their guano (very ammoniacal) or of their dermal gland secretions or by the noise of their late afternoon scrambling and squeaking, is often revealed instead by guano which sifts through cracks or is caught in cobwebs under cracks or accumulates in small piles in secluded corners. Even if a meticulous housekeeper has cleaned and cleaned, a short conversation (especially with the promise of removing some of the bats) usually elicits an account of where guano has been found on previous days. Then only ladders, ropes, and/or acrobatics are needed to capture a sample of the population.

My most peculiar adventure in capturing molossids occurred in 1956 while I was a guest at a Belgian-sponsored research station in Uvira on the banks of Lake Tanganyika. An inspection party consisting of the premier of Belgium, M. Spaak, and his associates, was expected for lunch one day. Feeling that it would be best if I were to keep out of the way during the preparations, I spent the morning exploring the enormous attic of the laboratory building. I became engrossed in what was an interesting biological situation. Two barn owls lived in the spacious attic and apparently fed, in part, on bats. Owl pellets, the regurgitated fur and bones of their prey, lay everywhere and I spent several hours identifying their victims. Not until almost noon did I spot a small colony of bats scurrying and playing in a far corner, under the eaves.

In my excitement to reach them before they were able to hide, I rushed across the attic beams, tripped on a nail-head, lost my footing, and stepped full force onto a thin beaverboard panel which made up the ceiling of the room below. I plunged through and landed in the middle of the festive buffet table which had been laid out for the enjoyment of M. Spaak and his party. Not only did I fall on and crush an uncertain number of delicacies but I carried with me a supply of guano which had been lying dry and dusty on the upper side of the broken panel.

The buffet was totally destroyed.

After the initial shock subsided, another buffet was prepared, the damage was swept up, and I was forgiven my gaffe. However, a large, man-shaped hole in the ceiling remained to glare mysteriously at the distinguished guests who arrived shortly thereafter for the luncheon.

Some ten years later, I joined a dinner party at Yale in honor of a visiting Belgian conservationist. In the course of our casual conversation, I discovered that he had been the governor of Ruanda-Urundi in 1956 and had been among the guests on the day of my ceiling penetration. He recalled quite spontaneously having been puzzled by the strange hole in the ceiling but had been far too well-mannered to make inquiry. My confession was the first he had heard of that day's events.

THE STORY OF MISS X

I have studied many pteropodid genera, including all of those believed to be closely related to *Rousettus* but none of which orient acoustically as *Rousettus* do. Since it seems unlikely that nocturnal fliers would have surrendered a sonar system, we may conclude that *Rousettus* have evolved such a system independently. I have studied three species of *Rousettus* and all orient alike. I was surprised to find, therefore, when I first captured a bat which I took to be *Rousettus angolensis*, that it oriented by vision and not by sound.

This Congolese bat had been the product of a time-consuming and exhausting field trip. We had driven half a day over a one-lane dirt road (one way in alternate directions on alternate days). Then, from the middle of nowhere, we walked for hours along barely visible foot trails to a village called Beshokwe.

A rather urbane-looking man, who turned out to be an itinerant tailor and scribe, was operating a sewing machine in the central square. He fulfilled for me a long established dream. I had always enjoyed sending my friends postcards from remote places with trivial messages in obscure tongues. Until that day, however, I had been frustrated by the linguistic acumen of these friends or of sources available to them. They could always decipher my cards. This man, however, responded to my inquiries by telling me that the local language was called Bongo-Bongo and that, as far as he knew, it was spoken only locally and had no written form, literature, or dictionary. He obligingly transliterated from French to Bongo-Bongo my dictated message "Having a wonderful time. Wish you were here." I dutifully copied this out onto several postcards. No one has ever deciphered them.

We reached the cave for which we were looking after another short hike and found it to contain some 20 brown pteropodids. I checked these against the most authoritative list of the bats of the Belgian Congo. Their gross appearance conformed exactly with the description of *Rousettus angolensis*. I knew, however, that they could not be *Rousettus* since they did not echolocate. Indeed, they were totally silent.

In consequence, I decided to bring one of these bats, soon named Miss X, back to Harvard with me alive. She proved to be an enchanting and long-term pet. Airlines are usually unwilling to allow bats aboard in the passenger compartment and most flights in those days did not have heated or pressurized cargo compartments. I regularly smuggled Miss X and a companion, *Rousettus aegyptiacus*, aboard in an overnight bag. They were detected only twice. Once, at the airport in Usumbura, in what is now Burundi, a cat made the discovery as we all waited (all but the cat) to board a flight. He took such a persistent interest and caused the bats such dismay (which they expressed by loud fluttering and squawking) that I had to retreat to the men's room in order to escape attention. In Leopoldville, as I climbed out of the taxi at my hotel, a bellhop, in the universal style of bellhops, grabbed my hand baggage, including the overnight bag, before I could interfere. His efficiency was repaid by his becoming increasingly aware that the bag was alive. It moved and thumped. By the time we reached my room, he had developed what can only be described as a distaste, if not a phobic fear, for this bag. He did not even wait for a tip!

I, too, suffered some discomfort from Miss X and her companion. Large bats of this type are quite noisy at night. They rendered sleep difficult when they shared my room even though I would often place them in their bag in a closet or in a dresser drawer to deaden their squawks and scrambling. The wooden walls unfortunately would then serve as sounding boards. We would all fall asleep as the sun rose, the bats by their endogenous activity rhythm and I in gratitude.

Back at Harvard, I consulted Barbara Lawrence, the curator of mammals, on the identity of Miss X. She assured me that it was *Rousettus angolensis* while I assured her that it could not be. The consequence of my obstinacy was that Miss Lawrence and I, after careful anatomical (on other specimens, not on Miss X) and behavioral assessment, created a new genus, *Lissonycteris*, for Miss X. She is now known as *Lissonycteris angolensis*.

OF BATS AND MEN

Bats consume enormous quantities of insects. They do not, of course, direct their attention particularly to what we consider to be harmful or noxious insects but nevertheless include a proportion of them in their diet. Mosquitoes, for example, and other biting flies, termites, and crop-consuming beetles and moths are preyed upon by bats. We owe a debt of gratitude to these dynamic insecticides. I have referred to estimated total catches elsewhere. In the laboratory, I have observed catch rates of up to two fruitflies per second though sustained rates come closer to 15 per minute.

An ingenious entrepreneur, some years ago, offered bat colonies, complete with houses, for sale to orchard owners. He promised that the bats would live in their owner's orchard and consume pests such as the apple codling moth. The scheme was not a success. We know of no way to keep bats in manmade homes once they are allowed freedom and we know even less of how to make bats choose particular insects for their diet.

The role of tropical bats in seed dispersal and pollination is probably more important than their consumption of insects. Many tropical plants have fruit designed to be attractive to bats. The fruit is not only borne in accessible locations, usually away from the bulk of the leaves and twigs, but is also green or brown, musty or unpleasant-smelling to men and has either large and inedible or small and slippery seeds. Bats often carry pieces of these fruits to their roost for leisurely chewing, thus dispersing the seeds. Large seeds are dropped after being cleansed of the surrounding pulp and small seeds are expectorated.

In the tropics, large groups of bats often inhabit homes, barns, and other buildings where they make themselves unwelcome by producing guano, by being noisy, or by their concentrated odor. Bat-proof architecture has reached a high degree of efficiency in some tropical countries. Indeed, in recent years in Jamaica, I have routinely avoided searching for bats in modern buildings or in buildings that appeared to have been recently remodeled. Local expertise is competent to exclude bats.

In temperate climates, older homes are more vulnerable, chiefly because they are likely to have shutters, loose roof- or wall-shingles, or unscreened ventilating louvers leading into the attic or into space under the roof. I have never seen a colony large enough in a house in a temperate climate, however, to cause the owners realistic distress. Nevertheless, I am plagued by letters and calls from people asking advice on how to rid their home of bats. Usually they have seen a single bat which probably strayed in through the chimney. I know of no way to bat-proof a house other than to rebuild it without interstices, so I advise these people to read about bats and to learn to value them as they would birds or other wildlife. One man called me not long ago to tell me of his home, completely and expensively covered with hand-hewn cedar shingles from the ground up. He claimed that he had counted several hundred bats emerging from behind the shingles on one side of the house alone. I encouraged him to add an appreciative aesthetic attitude toward bats to the pleasure he exhibited about the house.

Bats, like other animals, suffer illnesses. These seem not particularly common or severe, as witnessed by their longevity. With one exception, bat illnesses are not known to be shared with men. That exception is rabies, to which all mammals, including bats, are susceptible. We do not know whether bats (except for vampires) are significant in the transmission of rabies or play a role as reservoirs for the virus, but they appear not to be an important part of the epidemiology of the disease. Some years ago, a series of articles in an American magazine, later reprinted as a book with a sinister silhouette of a bat on the cover, focused on bats and rabies. These articles have done immeasurable harm. The number of cases of rabies in men which can be reasonably attributed to transmission from bats is perhaps one in the medical history of the United States. There may even have been two or three—still hardly a public health menace. More people die each year of black-fly bites, bee stings, or from contaminated food consumed at church suppers.

Vampires are known to be vectors of rabies in Mexico and in Trinidad. The scope of the problem, however, is hard to define. Few adequate observations have been made of other vectors such as foxes and skunks. Even in Mexico and in Trinidad, the alleged victims of vampire-borne rabies are cattle, not men.

Bats produce only one important commercial product— guano. The guano (urine and feces) of insectivorous bats is rich in nitrogen and is still used commercially as agricultural fertilizer in many tropical countries where an adequate chemical fertilizer industry is lacking. Dry caves with large, established bat populations may have many meters of guano on the floor, often, incidentally, hiding and preserving anthropologically interesting artifacts. The guano is mined, bagged, and marketed. At least until the time of the Castro government, there was a Cuban Bat Guano Corporation, for example.

Bats have had little use as aesthetic objects in and of themselves. Until recently, most bats had proved hard to maintain in captivity. Flying foxes and *Rousettus*, however, have been kept in European zoos since the mid-19th century and have also been house pets to some degree during the same period. In fact, Konrad Lorenz, the ethologist, tells of having had a pet flying fox as a boy. He would exercise it in the hallway of his home by launching it into the air and having it fly to the other end where it would land on his governess. The bat, was, of course, too large to be able to turn in the hallway and Lorenz could not safely exercise it outside.

A few people keep bats as pets. The late Ernest Walker, onetime curator of mammals of the Washington Zoo, for example, used to keep big brown bats as house pets. In the tropics, I have occasionally given favorite bats to families which had become enamored of them and all were reported to be rewarding and endearing pets. Most bats, however, require specialized care. Insectivorous bats may be fed mealworms (*Tenebrio*) which are the larvae of flour beetles. The mealworms themselves must be well fed since the bats, of course, depend on them for their nutrients. We keep our mealworms in a pan of dry Wheatena and add a slice of raw potato, a lettuce leaf, or a piece of firm banana from time to time for moisture and vitamins. Bats should also have a vitamin and mineral supplement and a water source.

In captivity, most bats take water from a dish without training. A few never learn to do so and have to be given water by hand daily. Some frugivorous species get an adequate water supply in their food and never drink water. In fact, I tested my belief that Miss X, my pet *Lissonycteris*, never took water by not offering her any for eight months. She thrived.

In nature, many bats can be seen dipping low over streams or ponds and touching the surface. We believe they are drinking but the details of how they do so are still poorly known. Other bats may capture raindrops or lap up moisture from rocks or vegetation. Of course, the insects which they prey upon also are likely to have water in their gut as well as in their tissues.

Feeding in captivity

Most insectivorous bats do well in captivity on a mixture called "glop," which has equal portions of mealworms, hardboiled egg yolk, cream cheese, and ripe, peeled banana blended with a few drops of a vitamin preparation. Glop is kept frozen since it spoils rapidly. Frugivorous bats in captivity will usually accept ripe banana and fresh or frozen melon. A few genera will eat other fresh, frozen, or preserved fruit such as pineapple.

At Yale we house our bats in a chamber which imitates a tropical cave. The room, about $5 \times 3.5 \times 2.5$ m, is large enough to allow all but the largest bats to fly freely. It is made of concrete blocks coated with plastic and is completely washable. There are no windows (other than a one-way observation window). The door, made of canvas with a zippered closure, is designed to avoid crushing errant bats. We have a choice of darkness and far red or white light. Temperature and humidity can be narrowly regulated and are ordinarily set at 80°F and 70-80 % R. H. All those bats which can be trusted are allowed full freedom in the room. Some which do not feed properly or fight are kept in large cages.

Bats have by now proved to be satisfactory laboratory animals for specialized purposes. But because of the expense of their care and their low reproductive rate, I do not expect them to become generally useful as experimental subjects.

33

THE WINGS

The ancestors of bats were almost certainly quadrupedal in posture and gait. What intermediate stages of locomotion they went through before they achieved winged flight is hard to imagine; possibly one of the stages was gliding in the manner of flying squirrels.

Only two other groups of flying vertebrates have ever evolved: birds, which have wings consisting of large quills taking rise from the edge of the forearm and from a severely reduced hand; and the extinct reptilian pterosaurs, which had wings of heavy skin extending from the side of the body to the arm and wrist and then along an enormously elongated fourth finger. Both of these groups, birds and pterosaurs, descended from the same group of reptilian ancestors which also gave rise to the dinosaurs and the crocodiles. A strong tendency toward bipedalism is apparent throughout these groups. A bipedal posture and gait leaves the front limbs available, evolutionarily, for uses other than weight bearing. In birds and pterosaurs, the use to which the front limbs were almost universally put was flight; few other functions, such as social signaling or sheltering of the young, are (or were) subserved.

Birds generally have well developed hind limbs adapted for walking and upright roosting. Many of the necessary modifications for balancing on these limbs had already been accomplished by their bipedal reptilian ancestors. Pterosaurs generally had rather poorly developed hind limbs but enormous wing expanses. Their proportions suggest that they were unable to walk or to roost upright. Instead, the pterosaurs probably hung suspended by their toe-claws from rocky outcroppings of cliff faces and engaged in a soaring type of flight. Their food sources and mode of feeding are not known and we cannot easily picture how they would have taken flight from the ground or from the surface of water if they landed.

Like pterosaurs, bats have wings that are made of skin, are attached to the sides of the body and are supported by the arms and fingers. The principal obvious difference in the wing design of bats and pterosaurs is the incorporation of the bats' fingers into the membrane in such a way as to provide a mechanism for governing the shape and tension of the wing.

The loss or partial loss of the ability of the forelimb-wings to function as limbs has in many genera imposed special restrictions on roosting, food manipulation, maternal care, and many other features of mammalian life, and these restrictions are expressed in alteration in behavior. The specialization of the wings for flight also imposes changes in general body architecture as well as in the structure and function of the hind limbs. The versatility of the wings and their uses are discussed in other chapters, in connection with locomotion, roosting, feeding, social behavior, and of course flight. In this chapter we will examine the construction of these curiously evolved limbs.

MOBILE THUMBS, BENT WINGS

All living bats and all fossils recognized as bats have essentially the same wing design. The animal's upper arm is relatively short and stoutly built; the forearm is long and slender. The small bones of the wrist are markedly reduced in number. The thumb bears a claw and is not much modified from the typical mammalian form though it may, as in flying foxes, be rather elongate. The thumb, like that of primates, is also exceptionally mobile. The other digits are markedly elongate. Each digit, second to fifth, consists of a metacarpal and two or three phalanges. The second finger forms, beyond the forearm, the leading edge of the wing. Its metacarpal is long but the phalanges may be quite short and the phalangeal joints relatively immobile.

The third finger, nearly always the longest, is placed almost immediately behind the second, where it helps to support the wing's leading edge as well as control its length and posture. The extra length of this finger usually requires rather intricate folding of the joints when the bat is at rest. (In the Old World genus, *Miniopterus*, the third finger is so long and so conspicuously folded when at rest that the group is known as bent-wing bats.) The fourth and fifth fingers, also long but usually not as long as the third, are well spaced out from each other and from the third. They serve as struts to support and to control the shape of about half of the wing membrane.

The wing membrane extends between the fingers and continues beyond the fifth to the side of the body and the leg, often as far down as one of the toes. Thus the rather triangular wing is bounded anteriorly by the arm, forearm, index, and third fingers; medially it is bounded by the body and leg; laterally it has a free edge supported only by the tips of the third, fourth, and fifth fingers. Usually a narrow membrane extends along the anterior edge of the forearm and upper arm as well, extending the wing somewhat anteriorly. Often there is also an interfemoral membrane between the legs, formed very much like the wings.

In two genera of bats, *Pteronotus*, a mustache bat, and *Dobsonia*, a relative of the flying foxes, the wings actually meet each other in the middle of the back, taking origin from the mid-line rather than from the sides of the body. Both of these bats, especially *Dobsonia*, look "naked" since the wings conceal or partly conceal the normally furred body. (A dress style of several years ago, the "trapeze," bore an uncanny resemblance to *Pteronotus*.)

Wingspread naturally varies with body size. The Philippine bamboo bat, *Tylonycteris pachypus*, the smallest known member of the order, weighs about 1.5 grams and has a wingspread of about 15 or 16 centimeters (6-6 ½ inches). Many of the common bats of North America which weigh about 4 to 15 grams have spreads of 25 to 30 cm. The largest of the flying foxes is said to have a spread of about 1.5 or even 1.7 meters (over 5 feet). I have measured in life the wingspread of the large Philippine flying fox, *Pteropus vampyrus*, and have found it to be about 130 cm.

Wing proportions also vary with family and genus. In some, length or spread is achieved by a longer forearm and/or index and third fingers. Many molossids and emballonurids have exaggerated wingspreads of this design, which seems to be associated with swift straight flight in open spaces. These bats usually maneuver relatively poorly but are powerful fliers. In other groups, the spread is conservative but the depth or width of the wings is increased by longer fourth or fifth fingers. This design allows slow or hovering flight and makes for greater maneuverability. Many of the horseshoe, leaf-nosed, and spear-nosed bats fall into this category.

THE SEERSUCKER PRINCIPLE

The wing membrane itself is made up almost entirely of an upper and a lower layer of skin. Between these layers is a small amount of connective tissue through which run fine blood vessels to nourish the skin and fine nerve trunks to innervate sense organs and smooth muscle fibers. Bundles of smooth muscle are, of course, incorporated into the blood vessel walls. In addition, hundreds of tiny aggregates of muscle are associated with special connective tissue so placed as to gather the skin into regular puckers as the fingers and arms fold. Much of the slack which would otherwise occur in the process of folding the membranes is immediately taken up by this seersucker-like puckering.

The wings are not known to have any special sense organs, only proprioceptors and detectors for touch, pressure, temperature and pain. (Until the discovery of bats' echolocation systems, scientists and laymen alike often attributed their nocturnal navigating skill to delicate nerve endings in the skin of the wings and of the face even though Spallanzani showed, as long ago as the 1790's, that individuals deprived of cutaneous sensation oriented well in flight.) The wings also include the bones, muscles, and tendons of the second, third, fourth, and fifth fingers. Indeed, the skin of the wing is often transparent enough to allow one to study the anatomy and distribution of the muscles and tendons of the hand by inspection. Even the muscles of the arm and forearm can often be seen and individually distinguished. One can easily recognize a juvenile bat, even after it has achieved essentially adult stature, by examining the finger bones: their ends are cartilaginous—translucent and rather knobby in appearance.

CONTROLLED CIRCULATION

The picture on the opposite page shows three major blood vessels coursing through the wing. The volume of blood circulating in the wings can probably be physiologically controlled, thus providing nutrition necessary to the tissues but avoiding excessive heat loss, heat gain, or dessication from the extensive skin expanse. Perhaps to insure an uninterrupted blood supply or perhaps for reasons of weight and bulk distribution, most of the finger-moving musculature is placed far medially while only long, fine tendons, which are light, non-bulky, and require very little blood supply, reach out to the bones that are being moved. The wing membranes are almost always deeply pigmented, dark brown or black. Occasionally, however, they are pinkish, white, or other pale shades. We do not known the function of this pigmentation.

The upper arms and forearms are often furry though sometimes more sparsely so than the body as a whole. In some genera, the fur spreads irregularly onto the nearby upper surface of the wing membrane, along the wrist, and sometimes beyond the wrist to the closest parts of the hand. I believe that the function of this kind of furring is related not to flying but to roosting. For example, very little fur is ever found on the under surface of the wings of bats where, of course, it could serve no purpose when the wings were folded. The distribution and the color pattern of wing fur tend to make the folded wings blend with the body, both to provide camouflage and to conserve heat. In bats which roost outdoors but do not fold their wings away, furring is either not seen or it is of minor degree. Fur over the entire surface of the wings might interfere with function, perhaps by making cleanliness difficult to maintain, perhaps by impairing aerodynamic qualities.

DANGER: WING INJURY

Obviously wing injuries are very serious matters for bats. Injuries are likely to result from intraspecific fights, desiccation, or collisions with obstacles such as thorns.

Fights are avoided; they are largely replaced by sham battles. In colonial species the wings are protected from accidents by being folded and tucked away. Bats often seem to avoid desiccation by selecting humid roosts. They generally avoid collisions by invoking a good sonar system, though some collisions do occur and serious wounds may ensue. Plants which are adapted for having their fruit taken and their seeds dispersed by bats, or for being pollinated by bats, ordinarily make provision for helping the bats avoid injury by holding the fruit or flowers in accessible positions.

In laboratory flight chambers, bats may collide with obstacles and often do so when flying test courses, skinning or bruising their forearms or fingers. Because of the poor vascularity (or circulation of blood) of the wings, these injuries are slow to heal. In captivity as well as in nature, however, many bats fly and feed successfully even after serious wing injuries such as substantial tears or fractures of some of the phalanges. We have often captured a healthy-looking bat with old, well-healed but once serious wing wounds. A fracture of the forearm or upper arm or an injury to the elbow or wrist joint, however, is normally rapidly fatal.

I believe that bats have a rather high pain threshold and will attempt to fly and will succeed in flying as long as the injury does not actually interfere mechanically with flight. By doing so they can survive the period required for healing to take place. In fact, flight *per se* may increase vascularity sufficiently to speed the healing process.

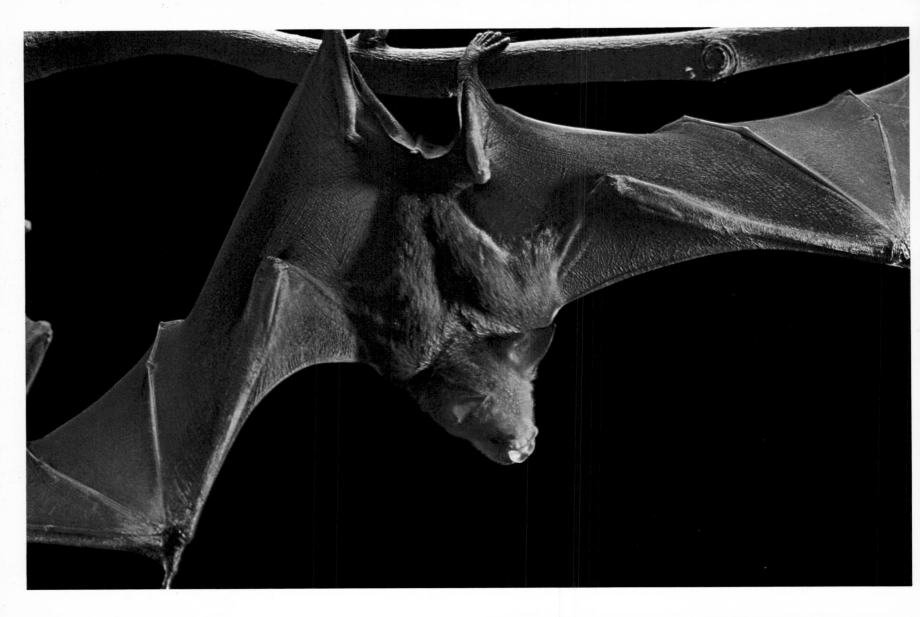

"FITTING" THE WINGS

A giant African leaf-nosed bat, *Hipposideros commersoni gigas*, has opened its wings *(above)*. The skin looks "fitted" because of its elastic quality, even on those parts of the wings that are not fully extended. At right, one wing has temporarily fallen into loose folds which will disappear when the wing is either fully spread or completely closed. The fact that the interfemoral membrane hangs loosely suggests that it is less elastic than the wing membrane, presumably because it plays a different role in a bat's life.

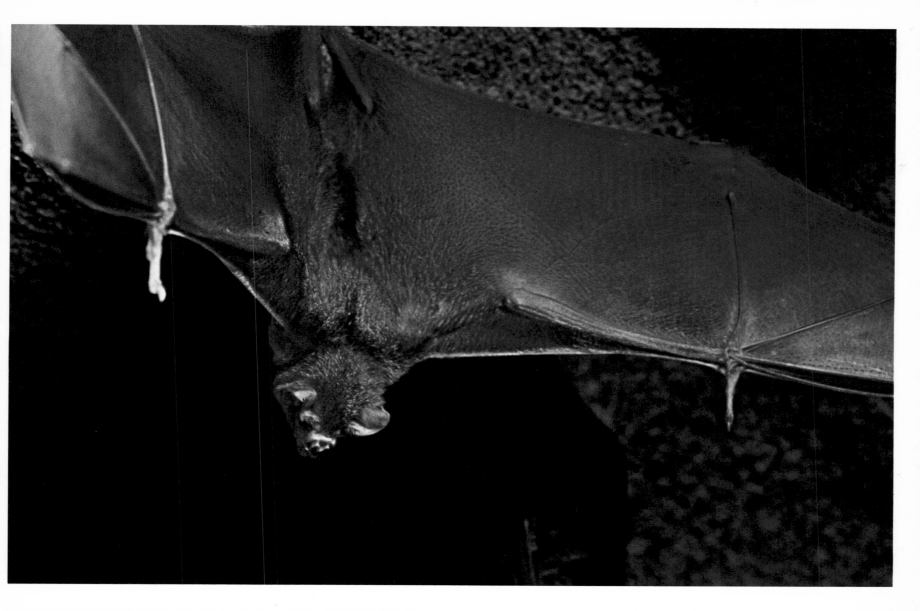

This picture of a vampire with wings fully spread *(top)* shows how the wing membrane of bats extends anteriorly from the arm and is reinforced by a sturdy, thickened forward edge. When using the wings as legs in quadrupedal movement, the vampire can fold them to the impressive degree seen at the left.

This group of flying foxes roosts with the fingers of the hands folded. At grooming time *(below, right)*, a folded wing has been stretched out for cleaning and oiling. As the wing membranes are stretched, visible changes in texture and tautness take place.

The effect of elastic connective tissue which gathers up or yields skin as a wing is closed or opened is visible as fine plications and striations at left in the wing membrane of the lump-nosed bat, *Plecotus rafinesqui.*

The partly folded wing of a dog-faced bat shrinks by changing into a rugose texture—i. e., by wrinkling.

THE HANDS IN THE WINGS

Here the unmistakeably hand-like structure of bat wings is strikingly demonstrated. On the bat's right is the free thumb and the webbed second, third, fourth and fifth metacarpal bones—the latter being the ones which would make up the palmar part of a man's hand.

The black, leathery skin of the wings of flying foxes is in strong contrast to the golden fur of the shoulders, which is in turn bordered by the shiny black fur of their backs. The black pigmentation of the wings may function as a shield against the carcinogenic effects of the sun's ultraviolet rays on bats which roost out in the open during tropical days, as flying foxes do.

Infant guano bats *(Tadarida brasiliensis mexicana)*, still unable to fly, nevertheless open their wings from time to time as they cling tenaciously to the nursery cave wall. The small wings, with immature bones that are partly cartilaginous and flexible, clearly resemble hands.

43

SPECTACULAR
AND BEAUTIFUL

The hoary bat, *Lasiurus cinereus*, is so densely furred and so cylindrical in shape (except for the wings) that its orientation is often confusing to the eye. The pictures on this page show back views of the bat in roosting positions. The skin of the wings, otherwise dark or speckled, shows orange areas along the forearm and fingers. The fur, generally frost-tipped brown, shades to a warmer yellow on the head and neck. The ears and nose are charmingly piped with black while tufts of cream-colored hair adorn the wrists and elbows. The combination of colors and shadings which the hoary bat rejoices in makes it, in the opinion of many, the most spectacular and beautiful bat of North America. But much more than esthetics is involved here, for the frost-tipped fur and the orange of the folded wings probably help conceal the animal when it roosts on lichen-covered tree trunks.

FUNCTIONAL
AND POWERFUL

Light is reflected glossily by the wings of *Noctilio leporinus*, the fishing bulldog bat of the Neotropics. These bats have wings that are uncommonly large in relation to the size of their body.

FLIGHT

The characteristics of flight in bats interact with a host of factors: their echolocation ability (or its absence); habitat; diet; roosting sites; size and weight; the details of their wing anatomy. Accordingly, we find wide variations in flight patterns and capabilities among bats.

The ways in which bats use their wings in flight are best conveyed by examination of the pictures in this and other chapters. Words cannot adequately describe the variety of positions and postures achieved by wings supported and shaped by the upper arm, forearm, and four fingers. Each finger consists of a metacarpal and two or three phalanges and each of these in turn is usually independently controlled. Bat wings may also be used either symmetrically or asymmetrically. They are employed somewhat differently in taking off, in landing, in descending, in ascending, in level flight, in hovering, and in an array of gymnastic movements such as dives, sharp turns, and somersaults.

In taking off from a hanging position, a bat first inspects its surroundings by sonar (or visually if the animal belongs to the suborder Megachiroptera). Then, in most cases, it simply releases its overhead hold, whether it be on a cave wall or ceiling or a branch. Some bats, however, especially the heavier species such as the flying foxes, flap their wings to raise the body to a more or less horizontal position before releasing their hold and taking off. Those inhabiting crevices or restrictive hollows in trees or very small side chambers in caves may have to crawl, jump, or scramble to an opening or ledge before they are able to take flight. And there are others which roost in such large clusters that only a few individuals are free to take flight at a given moment since there is literally no wing space for all of them at once.

As they approach a landing, those that can do so identify by sonar the place where they intend to hang. They then usually flip over in full flight, throw their claws against the roost, grasp it, and hang. In some cases, the surface of the rock may offer only faint irregularities but these are apparently readily identified in advance. Furthermore, they prove to be adequate anchorages.

Bats which are colonial in habit will generally seek out a landing perch already occupied by one or more colleagues. They often, perhaps usually, actually land on top of a colleague who as a rule quietly tolerates the sudden shock. Having landed, the newcomer reaches out and finds its own footholds. Whether bats locate their colleagues by echolocation or by smell or whether they sometimes home in on sonar signals being emitted by those already roosting has not been established. It is known that bats prefer to land and to roost in places that have previously been occupied by bats of their own species or, to a lesser extent, by some other compatible species. In our laboratory, free-flying bats will enter any previously occupied but empty cage and roost until morning. They will ignore clean cages.

RESETTING THE CLOCK

Most of the conspicuous bats of temperate climates leave their daytime roosts *en masse* at dusk and immediately begin their pursuit of insects. However, systematic observations of bat populations of tropical caves have shown that these species emerge more or less sequentially, often long past dark. In the case of Mount Plenty Cave in Jamaica, for example, *Monophyllus* are followed by *Chilonycteris* (first the small species *psilotis*, then the large *parnellii*). *Artibeus* and *Phyllonycteris* emerge later. In Mexico I have often noticed that vampires are the last to emerge, sometimes as late as 10 p.m.

Watching bats in tropical caves in late afternoon, one sees increasing preening and hears additional bickering and vocalizing towards dusk. Then, within the larger chambers, a few bats start flying great circles, during the course of which they pass one or more of the principal exits. More and more individuals are recruited to these circular flights until some hundreds or thousands of bats may be moving together in long swirls. Apparently, as they pass the exits they judge the intensity of light and decide whether to emerge or not. On dark, overcast evenings, bats emerge earlier. They also emerge earlier through exits which are deep in ravines or are heavily shaded than they do through exits which face the clear sky or open to the west. Their emergence time varies, of course, with the sunset. (I have found that a cave population can be substantially "bottled up" beyond sunset by placing a single flashlight in the cave exit, shining inwards.) Bats awaken in response to a built-in rhythm of activity such as has been demonstrated in a wide variety of other living organisms. Their flights past the lighted exits reset their internal clock if necessary and keep it synchronized with the solar day and night. That is, if the bat awakens too early, its clock is reset by its view of full daylight. The next night it sleeps longer and commences flying later. Flight within the cave may also help to synchronize members of the population with one another by shifting forward the activity cycles of late awakeners. In any event, flight within the cave would seem to serve the purpose of fully awakening each bat and bringing its metabolism and coordination up to full level before it emerges into a more challenging world.

Flying in a cave in this way, accompanied by a swirl of hundreds of companions, must create serious orientation problems. The noise level includes a multiplicity of odd reverberations of sound from the irregular facets of the walls and ceiling plus the orientation pulses and echoes of all the other bats. In order to echolocate effectively, a bat must be able to identify the echoes of its own pulses. I now believe that bats flying systematically in their own cave may do so largely by memory. They are exposed repeatedly to the same, essentially unchanging geometry. To memorize this configuration ought not to be a major challenge. In addition, in several experimental situations we have observed what D.R. Griffin has called the "*Andrea Doria* effect"*: bats may have their sonar turned on but in familiar locations they apparently navigate by custom, paying no attention to the echoes. If obstacles are unexpectedly introduced into the environment, the bats crash into them even while producing normal sonar signals.

PATTERNS BY SPECIES

Once they emerge from their roosts, bats fly to their hunting grounds and begin to feed. They may stop to drink *en route* or may drink later, while feeding. Many species of bats seem to have habitual hunting trails but unfortunately our information on flight activity after emergence is sparse. Bats are hard to see and even harder to identify by species in the dark. Even when we see bats in flight, we rarely know whence they came or where they are headed. Some individuals are known to have favorite hunting grounds such as a clearing in the woods, over a pond, or near a farm house. Others, principally frugivorous species, are known at times to cover

* An allusion to the collision of the liner of this name in 1956 with the *Stockholm*, which took place in the Atlantic not far from New York City and which sank the *Andrea Doria*. Both ships of course had radar which should have warned of the danger.

some distance in order to reach a certain grove of trees in flower or with ripening fruit. From scattered anecdotal reports, we can estimate that some species of bats feed almost entirely within a few hundred yards to a mile of their daytime roosts. Others may cover slightly greater distances and some may fly as much as 30 miles or more each way. *Rousettus*, for example, converge on the naval base at Sangley Point in the Philippines at certain seasons to feed on ripening fruit there even though no *Rousettus* colonies have ever been discovered within 20 miles or more.

Insectivorous bats may fly at species-characteristic altitudes. Thus some skim along just above the vegetation, some at 6 or 10 meters (20 to 32 feet) from the ground. There are those, particularly large free-tailed bats, that are said to fly at 300 meters (about 1000 feet) or even more. Presumably flight altitudes are set to coincide with the flight altitudes of preferred prey species.

Insectivorous bats also have preferred flight terrains. They may hunt exclusively beneath or above the jungle canopy, above the savannah, in clearings in the forest, or only in completely open air, well above any vegetation. Not only flight pattern but wing anatomy and sonar design are involved in such specializations. Bats which fly swiftly and straight usually fly over open country at fair to high altitudes and have long and narrow wings. They are relatively poor at changing course in a small space and relatively clumsy when flying in caves or otherwise confined. Finding it difficult or impractical to take off from the ground or under cluttered conditions such as are imposed by underbrush, they often roost in and take off from elevated places. These bats also usually use very intense and high frequency-modulated orientation pulses.

The intensity presumably is designed to increase their effective inspection range in an environment in which echoing surfaces are rare. Bats of this type have been observed to fly at speeds of perhaps 5 or 6 meters per second or 10 to 12 miles per hour. We lack reliable data since flight speed is hard to measure in nature and may well be altered in captivity. This type of bat flight may involve 6 or 8 wing beats per second.

Bats which fly in jungle thickets usually have relatively short, broad wings and fly slowly, even hovering in place when necessary. They generally produce sonar signals of low intensity and short duration, often lacking frequency modulation. Similar wing, flight, and sonar patterns characterize bats which seek insects on vegetation or on the ground; those which are carnivorous; and those which feed on flowers or fruit, even when they fly in relatively open country. The forward flight speed of these bats varies but is typically slower than that of the group described above. A reasonable guess would be about 1 to 3 meters per second.

FAINT SONAR, SLOW FLIGHT

Short broad wings seem adapted to slow flight, quick changes in direction, and hovering. In a jungle, the presence of a very large number of obstacles makes it more difficult to detect and pursue food objects. The use of sonar signals of low intensity avoids the reception of echoes from too many objects because it restricts inspection to the immediate vicinity. A bat's ability to resolve a complex pattern of echoes is necessarily finite; presumably in complex environments some exclusion of postponable information is desirable. Unless

The ghost drawing at left corresponds to the right-hand half of the fold-out, and shows these bats, as numbered:

18. Macrotus waterhousii
19. Antrozous pallidus
20. Leptonycteris sanborni
21. Monophyllus redmani
22. Leptonycteris sanborni
23. Hipposideros commersoni gigas
24. Pteropus giganteus
25. Carollia sp.
26. Rousettus aegyptiacus
27. Noctilio leporinus
28. Artibeus jamaicensis
29. Euderma maculatum
30. Macrotus waterhousii
31. Macrotus waterhousii
32. Pteropus giganteus

these bats fly slowly, however, collisions will occur with some of the more distant objects before they are identified. Thus low sonar intensity goes with slow flight. Short pulse duration is also characteristic of almost all sonar systems when the bat is very close to its target, a situation which prevails most of the time in the jungle or among bats that hunt along walls, trees, or near the ground. Short pulses avoid or minimise the frequency of long overlaps at the bat's ear between outgoing pulses and returning echoes.

Though insectivorous bats hunting in clearings or over ponds often display the erratic flight paths that have made them symbols of inconstancy, fickleness, or of an erratic nature, a bat's uninterrupted flight path is straight and true. These are the paths followed by bats flying to or from feeding grounds or when they fly in large caves. In the field, each change in direction, each dive, somersault, or sideslip indicates pursuit and usually capture of an insect. (We have no data on the proportion of pursuits which are successful in nature.) The bat alters its path to intercept each insect which it detects and assesses as desirable. When capturing insects at the rate of one or two per second, a bat will naturally appear to be flying erratically because of the braking and accelerating that are required. The short flights between insect pursuits are straight or gently curved.

During the night, many bats, having fed, will hang up at a nocturnal roost to rest or sleep while digesting their catch. Such night roosts can often be recognized by the heaps of discarded food fragments found there or by their discrete guano heaps—each representing the habitual return of a single bat to a specific site such as a branch or a rocky overhang. In many species, such a nocturnal rest is followed by another foraging flight. Eventually the bat returns to its diurnal roost. In some cases, fully fed bats may be seen returning to their caves by 10 or 11 p.m. In other cases they may be out most of the night but almost invariably return before dawn.

MIGRATION

In addition to flying for food, bats also engage in long-distance, seasonal, migratory flights to and from hibernation sites and other over-wintering areas, and to or from nursery colonies and fresh foraging areas. Flights of these kinds have been well documented by naturalists in North America, Europe, and Australia as ranging from 50-100 miles up to 1500 miles or more. In general, the data are derived from banding records of bats that have been captured, banded, and released. Later recoveries make possible the reconstruction of a movement map. In New England, for example, bats of several species retreat to Mount Aeolus in Vermont from diverse summering sites in all directions and at substantial distances. We know very little of the mechanics or details of such flights. How, for example, do bats provision for such flights or do they feed *en route*? How do they navigate and how do they recognize their goal? How is the direction chosen, one way in the fall, another way in the spring, and what triggers the movements (which are normally quite synchronous and efficient)? Is there a leader? No answers are yet available.

Recently several investigators have reopened the question of whether migrating bats may navigate visually by the use of landmarks or the constellations. At first, the idea is startling. Scientists have tended to ignore vision in bats endowed with

The ghost drawing at right corresponds to the left-hand half of the fold-out, and shows these bats as numbered:

1. Vampyrum spectrum
2. Monophyllus redmani
3. Noctilio leporinus
4. Artibeus jamaicensis
5. Macrotus californicus
6. Leptonycteris sanborni
7. Vampyrum spectrum (carrying a mouse)
8. Carollia sp.
9. Artibeus jamaicensis
10. Macrotus waterhousii
11. Artibeus sp.
12. Hipposideros commersoni gigas
13. Hipposideros commersoni gigas
14. Desmodus rotundus murinus
15. Artibeus jamaicensis
16. Macrotus waterhousii
17. Monophyllus redmani

This dog-faced bat appears to be simulating a parachute. Close to the en of a down stroke, the wings are fully extended and symmetrical.

echolocation since it seems of so little day-to-day use and is clearly unnecessary for foraging flights. As noted previously, Spallanzani showed long ago that blinded bats did as well in nature as their sighted colleagues, as far as one could judge by their state of nutrition. Experimental probes of the use of vision in navigation, however, seem at the moment to be very promising.

Flight is necessary to sustain life in bats. Every mechanism for reducing weight must surely be favored and every load-increasing influence opposed. Bats usually eliminate wastes before taking flight and do so repeatedly during flight in order to hold down their nonfunctional load. Loads must also be centralized if possible and the body slung efficiently from the vertebral column and pelvis as is the case in birds.

TRAFFIC JAM AT DAWN

A graphic description of flight prowess by Mexican free-tailed bats has been published by three biologists* studying them in Texas caves, including Bracken Cave which is shown in photographs in the "Social and Family Life" chapter. Their observations of return flights to the cave showed that the first group might appear as early as 11 p.m. The flights increase gradually through the night, then begin tapering off by sunrise to intermittent groups and cease by the time the sun is above the horizon. Only occasionally do any returnees arrive as late as an hour after sun up. The build-up of the streams of bats returning is apparently quite dramatic. "The first incoming bats," they write, "seemed to approach the cave most leisurely, often in a long, shallow, zig-zag glide. As the

* Richard B. Davis, Clyde F. Herreid II, Henry L. Short. Their findings were published in Ecological Monographs, Volume 32, Number 4.

density of the flight increased, the approach angle steepened By the time the incoming stream became continuous the bat in it literally were dropping out of the sky into the mouth of the cave. Each bat was executing a rapid series of free falls with closed wings, punctuated by the abrupt, brief opening of its wings to control speed and direction.... Each brief braking action with wings open produced a muffled ripping sound so that the night was filled with an eerie staccato as the rain of dark shapes hurtled into the cave....

"On one occasion we witnessed a dawn traffic jam high in the sky above Bracken Cave. There were so many bats in the sky that they could not possibly all come in at once. The problem was resolved by the apparent establishment of a landing pattern to which all groups adhered. About ten large groups formed a loose, wide, wheeling circle at an altitude estimated as exceeding 6,000 feet. As one group pealed off to plummet down, another moved in from outside the circle to take its place. Groups arriving late made long lateral flights to await their turns in the circle, but they seemed to come back in perfect time to fill an opening. This orderly array was operating so rapidly that a continuous stream of bats was entering the cave below. Each group in this flight not only maintained its integrity but also oriented in recognition of the other groups.

"On several other occasions we overdid the job of blocking the mouth of the cave for the purpose of directing bats through our trap, and bats accumulated in the air outside the cave more rapidly than they could gain access. This confusion was quickly overcome by formation of wheeling circles of bats at tree top level just outside the cave. While the circle grew to accommodate bats falling from above, the circle developed an orderly tangential side stream just the right size to fit the available opening into the cave."

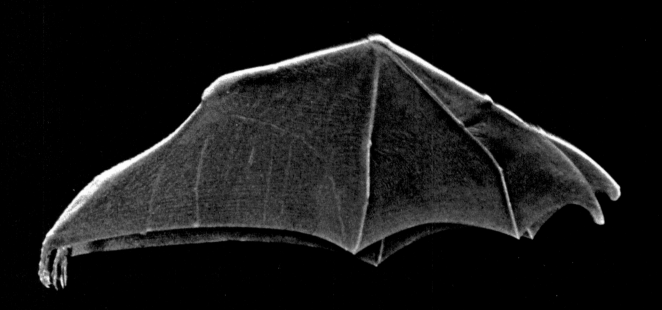

The dog-faced bat, *Rousettus aegyptiacus*, is seen here in postures which show that the legs and feet move during flight as well as the wings. Above, the bat's hips, knees and ankles are fully extended as the wings pass the top of an upstroke. At right, the knees are slightly flexed, the ankles relaxed.

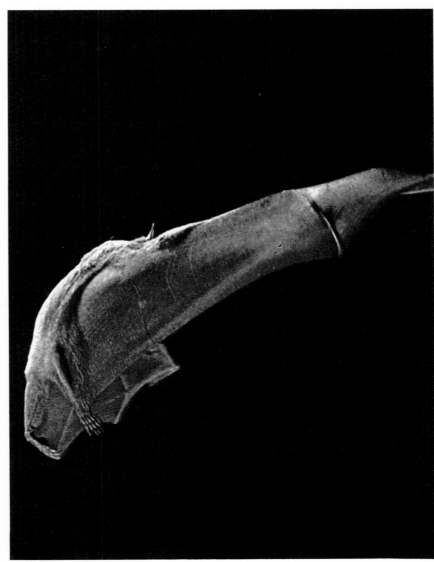

As the bat's wings stretch forward in a down stroke, its ankles flex *(left)*. In a view from behind, the feet are again flexed at the ankle *(above)*; in addition, they are also turned upward as the wings reach up and forward.

TAKE-OFF STYLES

The uppermost of these two vampires *(left)* is apparently considering a take-off from the wall on which they have been hanging. One wing is still completely folded while the other is outstretched in an "intention" movement which in effect signals what the bat is planning to do. It has raised its head and extended its neck in order to survey the surroundings by sonar. A moment later it may spread both wings and take flight.

When a dog-faced bat has been hanging from a branch with both feet on the same side and the toes pointed ventrally, the first step in taking off is simply to spread and flap the wings in order to raise the body to a horizontal position or higher *(above)*. Then the toehold is released and the bat is immediately in full flight *(left)*. If the toes had been clutching opposite sides of a branch, one foothold would have been released before the wings were spread.

THE LANDING "FLIP"

Two *Macrotus* roost on a forked branch while a third comes in to land. At top, the newcomer's left wing is already substantially folded as the left foot reaches out for the branch. The bat roosting at the fork may have been alerted to the approach, probably by sonar signals, and has turned towards the landing bat. In the second picture the newcomer has just made the so-called landing flip and come down on top of the one already there, knocking it partly aside. The landing animal's wings are not yet folded and it has not stabilized its position. A few moments later *(right)*, the newcomer is moving backwards up the branch, away from direct contact. A third bat, in the background, has been startled, probably by the jolt of the landing, and has momentarily begun to stretch its wings, ready to escape if necessary.

Here is a closer look at the landing flip, again performed by *Macrotus*. Above, in the middle of the flip, the bat's wings are in a beautifully asymmetrical position. The left foot has all but grasped the branch. Continuation of the flip will carry the right foot to its hold as well. Right, the bat is now securely settled but its wings are not yet folded. Most bats need to flip over in this way before grasping a foothold.

A TURNING MANEUVER

The bizárre wing posture revealed in this photograph of a dog-faced bat comes as a surprise even to a close observer of bat behavior. The left wing is in the normal position for a down stroke but the joints of the fingers of the other are hyperextended so that the under surface of the wing is literally convex—like an umbrella turned inside out by wind. This is probably part of a turning maneuver.

HOVERING

Hovering flight *(right)* as exhibited by the small Jamaican nectar feeder, *Monophyllus redmani*. The first joints of the fourth and fifth fingers are hyperextended. Thus the outer portion of each wing is canted differently from the center. The bat's open mouth suggests that its sonar signals are being emitted orally.

Below is *Monophyllus* in another hovering posture. In this case the left wing is held in much the same position as it is in the picture above, but the leading edge of the right wing has been pulled into a hairpin shape by strong flexion of the fourth and fifth fingers.

A big-eared bat in hovering flight *(above)* illustrates the degree to which the fingers and their various joints can be employed individually to produce any particular desired posture out of a large and varied repertory.

FINGERS AND ANKLES

Leptonycteris in a hovering posture while feeding from an agave flower. The hovering which is required for this kind of specialized feeding can be sustained for a long time.

A dog-faced bat *(left)* discovered in a startling flight posture: the forearm is held well up but the fingers are sharply flexed at the wrist. The net result is that the wings are in effect collapsed.

The off-center, turned head; the asymmetric wing positions; and the widespread legs of *Macrotus (right)*—all indicate that the bat is banking to turn or to land. In this genus, as in many others, the interfemoral membrane is supported not only by the two legs from the hips to the ankles but also by the tail in the middle and the elongated heel bones at the outside corners.

Flying foxes differ in their flight from most other bats because their wing spread and body weight are so much greater. They require considerable altitude and freedom from obstacles when taking off and thus usually choose elevated roosts in rather bare, tall trees well above the jungle canopy. These bats may regularly fly many miles from their daytime roosts to orchards or other sources of ripening fruit. In the open, when well above the ground, they may take advantage of air currents to soar. The variety of wing postures exhibited here is not unlike those of *Rousettus*

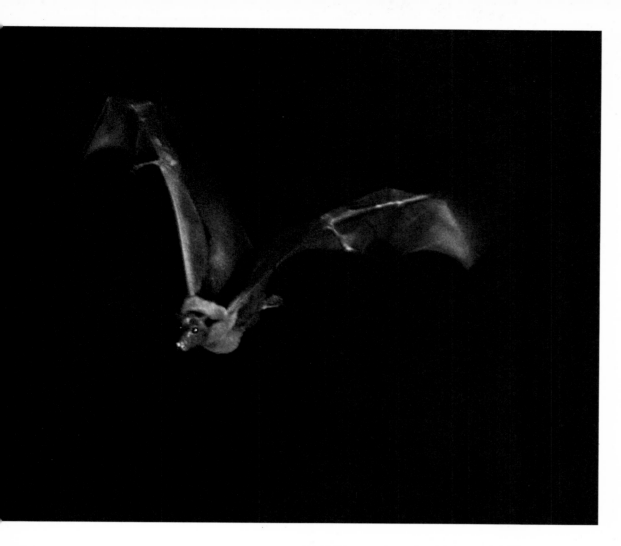

Noctilio, the fishing bulldog bat, is seen here in a series of flight maneuvers, some of them extremely graceful, as it flies down to skim the surface of a pool. In the picture above the fingers are intricately flexed while the body and head are carried parallel to the water.

As *Noctilio* flies over and parallel to the water, the legs dip down and the feet, with their unusually large claws, penetrate the surface. The wings are notably longer and narrower than those of non-fishing bats.

AN ADEPT MANEUVERER

Exceptionally wide wings make *Macrotus* an excellent maneuverer while flying through tight spaces or landing on and taking off from vegetation or the ground (where it is unable to walk). The picture at left shows the beginning of a take-off, with one wing already fully spread, the other still partly folded.

Macrotus in flight *(above and right)* deftly avoids brushing against any vegetation near its flight path.

With wings fully spread, *Macrotus* makes a gentle landing on a shrub, hardly disturbing the leaves. Then *(right)*, it takes off easily in a vertical flight path, using a symmetrical wing posture.

Leptonycteris are versatile fliers: they can hover, maneuver in tight spaces, and fly swiftly forward as well. Their wings are relatively short (in total spread) but broad (in finger length), proportions which hold true for most bats required to hover in their daily foraging flights.

Opposite: a group of Jamaican fruit bats, *Artibeus jamaicensis*, in confused flight. When many bats are startled into flight in a confined space, their echolocation ability is seriously hampered. The difficulty arises from the need of each bat to identify echoes from its own sonar pulses while screening out the echoes or pulses coming from other bats. Damaging collisions often occur at times like this.

Bats of the genus *Rousettus*, whose sonar signals are audible to man as a series of clicks, orient visually in the light, acoustically in the dark. If the light is turned off while a *Rousettus* is in flight in a room, on go the clicks. Conversely, when the light is switched on, the clicks stop as instantly as if the switch were operating the bat, not the light. The bat above is orienting acoustically, holding its lips apart as it emits the sounds.

SOCIAL AND FAMILY LIFE

In their propensity for communal living, bats vary enormously. Some species are gregarious almost beyond imagination; others are solitary. There are also numerous arrangements in between. Some species roost readily in proximity with other kinds of bats while others seem to shun such neighbors.

In many species, individuals come together to make up aggregates, known as colonies, during at least part of the year. The numbers can be huge. The summer nursery colonies of Mexican free-tailed bats *(Tadarida brasiliensis mexicana)* in several caves in Texas and New Mexico, for example, number in the millions. As noted earlier, as many as 20 million adult females plus their young have been observed in Bracken Cave near San Antonio. The so-called camps of flying foxes roosting in trees in the tropical Cape York peninsula of Australia may number two to four million individuals. The combined weight of a group of flying foxes has been known to break off sturdy tree limbs on which they were roosting.

I have seen a cave near Penonemé in Panama in which three species of mustache bats, *Chilonycteris* and *Pteronotus*, literally lined the wall and ceiling. No rock whatsoever was visible when I first entered this cave. In Rosario near Manila in the Philippines, I have observed a colony of at least tens of thousands of *Taphozous philippinensis*, a sheath-tailed bat, occupying a church belfry and open attic. In the Congo, thousands upon thousands of several species of free-tailed bats live in essentially every roof and attic in Kinshasa (formerly Leopoldville). Colonies of this kind are easy to locate, for in the late afternoon they can be heard from the street as they noisily bicker and play. In the course of doing fieldwork one also learns to recognize the presence of colonies by smell. Large colonies of this kind are formed by some genera of almost every family, and their roosts may be occupied to physical capacity.

Many bats form smaller colonies which vary from several dozen to several hundred at most. These have been found in parts of caves where there would seem to be plenty of room for larger groups. We do not know what it is that limits the population in this kind of situation. Bats which gather in small groups are not necessarily less common than those which gather by the tens of thousands. They may simply have a much greater number of roosting sites. The Jamaica fruit bat, *Artibeus jamaicensis*, for example, is common throughout most of tropical America, yet I have never seen more than a few hundred roosting in a single site (as it happens, an old hacienda in Paso de Ovejas, Mexico). This is true, as well, of the common vampire, *Desmodus rotundus*, the fishing bulldog bat, *Noctilio leporinus*, the big-eared bat, *Macrotus*, and the Neotropical funnel-eared bat, *Natalus mexicanus*. Bats which form such limited colonies may also occupy hollow trees, culverts, and other outdoor or semi-exposed sites as well as caves.

MILITANT LONERS

Some species appear to be militantly solitary in their roosting habits. I believe these to be much less abundant than those of the preceding groups but attempts to count them or even to estimate their population are frustrated by their distribution. Among the solitary species are the small Philippine bat, *Myotis jeannei*, the red bat and the hoary bat of North America, both *Lasiurus*, and the large African fruit bat, *Hypsignathus*. Being hard to find in quantity, solitary bats have been very little studied. Some are known to return not only to the same roost night after night but even year after year. They are apparently "attached" to their regular roost and able to locate and identify it on returning from foraging or from seasonal migrations. They may change roosts in a regular seasonal pattern, repeating the pattern year after year.

The reasons for roosting in large or in small colonies are by no means fully worked out. Large colony formation, in some cases, may be a seasonal affair. In many species, the females come from extended geographic regions to gather in special nursery caves to bear and rear their young. A case of this sort has been studied in detail in Australia. Here the nursery chamber was shown to be warmer than the premises occupied by males of the same species or by females at other seasons. The shape of the chamber helped to conserve heat which derived from the bodies of the bats as well as from the fermentation of their guano on the cave floor. One advantage of this arrangement is obvious: the young could be kept relatively warm at smaller metabolic expense to the mothers.

The mothers could also save energy in keeping warm themselves, perhaps to compensate for what they lost in lactation. Indeed, the processes of growth and lactation themselves may require higher body temperatures, the maintenance of which may be possible only in heated chambers. In other nursery colonies, "central heating" does not appear to be the prime concern. In colonies in tropical sunbaked sites, the young are sometimes put to play together. The advantage here may be the opportunity for exercise and companionship.

Many nurseries exclude not only males of the same species but other bats too, thus reducing the number of intruders that might deliberately or inadvertently injure the young or knock them from their roost. The young are of course small, relatively weak, and poor in coordination. In many cases, they have no way of climbing back to their mother if pushed to the floor. Cave floors are commonly covered by water; even when dry, they swarm with carnivorous insects.

In my laboratory I have several times observed the formation of a nursery colony by *Artibeus jamaicensis*. Forced to live in a room with other bats, the females when late in pregnancy took possession of a vacant roost which consisted of an old burlap potato sack hanging on the wall. They remained there, segregated from all other *Artibeus*, including non-productive females as well as males, and from bats of other species, until their young were weaned. Later, after the sack had been occupied for a while by Mexican free-tailed bats, *Artibeus* would no longer use it for child-bearing. Conceivably they did not like the odor of the free-tailed species.

One advantage of large colony formation is evident in the procedure that free-tailed bats follow in emerging from their roosts. In tropical cities, where countless buildings house large populations of molossids, one can hear them stirring, scrambling, and bickering in their roosts beginning a couple of hours before dusk. At about 15 minutes before dark, perhaps 6 or 6:15 p.m. near the equator and 7 p.m. in Jamaica in July, a group of about 20 to 50 individuals will gather just inside the structure at a take-off point. Then suddenly the members of the group all take flight together or as closely together as the shape of the structure and the aperture permit. For some yards they fly either in an expanding ball or in a short tight

stream. I call this emergence by *coup*. A minute or two may pass before another *coup*; then there is another and another until all the bats have emerged. The *coups*, appearing suddenly and having so many independently moving parts, make it very difficult for predators waiting outside and hunting by vision to fix on any one victim.

SEGREGATION BY SEX

Many bats segregate by sex. Mexican free-tailed males and females, for example, apparently meet only to mate. Otherwise they roost separately throughout the year. The females of the large cave colonies in Texas and New Mexico pass the winter in Mexico, often migrating 1500 miles or even more. In the spring, males and females both start north, encounter each other *en route* and mate in one-night roosts in buildings, caves, or hollow trees. Courtship is apparently short and the pair bond dissolved immediately. Not all the males migrate as far north as the females and they usually roost in small groups in buildings, crevices, and other obscure sites. In collecting both outdoor-roosting and cave-dwelling bats in a given chamber or tree or even in an entire cave, I have often found only males or only females, even outside of the child-bearing season. In New England during the summer, male vespertilionid bats such as *Eptesicus* and *Myotis* appear to be scattered and sparse while females are commonly found in groups in attics and barns. One advantage of segregation by sex may be to reduce competition between males and females for food. If so, I would predict that among those species in which the sexes are markedly different in size (and probably therefore in hunting habits) there might well be less sexual segregation. If the two feed on different insects or at different altitudes, their need to be separated may be reduced.

Species which hibernate may abandon seasonal segregation and form large colonies that include both sexes. *Eptesicus fuscus*, the big brown bat of North America, does this. Such colonies seem to serve at least three significant functions. First, large and tightly clustered aggregates conserve heat since only part of the surface of each bat is reached by the circulating air of the cave or touches the stone wall; the rest is pressed against the body of a neighbor. Second, reoccupation of a cave which has previously been a satisfactory hibernation site increases the likelihood of winter survival. The cave is presumably safe or at least safer than a randomly selected new roost would be. Third, these bats mate in their caves before entering hibernation. The egg is not immediately fertilized, however. Instead the sperm survive in the female's genital tract until early spring; only then does fertilization occur and implantation follow. This remarkable process allows sperm production to coincide with the male's nutritional peak. Gestation in the spring, on the other hand, occurs when the female is able to find an abundance of food and rapidly restore her own nutritional level as well as support her pregnancy. The young are also born and reared at a time when food is abundant and they can reach adulthood before winter again sets in.

While many colonial bats roost pressed one against the other, most of those which form smaller groups roost spaced out. What advantages might spacing bring? There are no solid answers to this question. Far from conserving heat, spacing out should provide for greater heat loss. But this is not as yet known to be required by any bat in its roost. *Macrotus waterhousii*, which regularly roost spaced out, succumb in captivity within a few hours if they are confined in close groups, while in spacious cages, with free air flow and freedom of movement, they are among the longest lived.

SOCIAL STRUCTURE OR TERRITORIALITY?

We know of no demonstrated cases of hierarchy formation in bat colonies or social structuring among individuals other than those of mothers and young or mating pairs. In my laboratory I have observed that among captive *Cheiromeles*, the giant Malaysian free-tailed bat, and vampires, for example, individuals may take up regular roosting positions relative to the other members of the colony. Among *Chilonycteris* there are also loose orders of feeding. *Pteropus*, in nature, bicker and shove at their roosts. These and similar observations do not necessarily prove the existence of a social structure. They ma simply demonstrate roost-site permanence, some degree c territoriality, or merely different levels of activity or differen personality traits among individuals. In a number of specie in captivity, especially *Hipposideros*, I have found males to b intolerant of the close approach of other males and I interpre this to be evidence of territoriality. The territory may consis of no more space then the individual's forearms can encompas

Some species of bats—vampires are a good example— always roost apart from all other bats. We do not know wh avoids whom. I have never seen *Natalus, Glossophaga, Saccop teryx, Rhinolophus,* or *Hipposideros* roosting with other specie They may use caves which house other bats but they alway hang separately. There are, however, species of bats which ar almost always found roosting together. *Chilonycteris, Pteronotu* and *Mormoops* (all Chilonycterinae) are often found in mixe clusters. They also join at times with *Leptonycteris, Phyllony teris,* and *Monophyllus.* We really know nothing of thes relationships or their significance.

COURTSHIP AND MATING

A wide variety of bats have large dermal glands, often o the face, chin, throat, or near the anus. These dermal gland sometimes vary with sex, maturity, or the sexual cycle of bat In other cases, glandular activity appears to be independer of sex and season. The secretions of some of these derma glands may be active in conditioning the skin and fur of bat The characteristic odors may also serve as species or se recognition signals. The odors, in addition, may be used offend other bats or other potential competitors so as to secu roost privacy; or they may mark off roosting territorie Finally, the odors may help bats when they must relocate the cave entrance or hollow tree in the darkness and in spite of confusing or complicated terrain.

Mating among animals, including bats, is usually precede by courtship which functions to identify, reciprocally, the ma and female as being of opposite sex and of the same specie In addition, participation in courtship, rather than withdraw or aggression, implies that both are mature and in a state of reproductive readiness. In mammals, females that are physiologically prepared for mating are said to be in estrous. In males, the equivalent state is sometimes called the rut.

In bats, adult females in general have a single estrous cycle per year, though some tropical species appear to have two. In temperate climates the cycle may occur in the fall, just preceding hibernation. In the tropics, the estrous cycle is generally synchronized with the seasons but the timing varies from species to species. During the course of the estrous cycle, the ovaries produce one or more eggs, the lining of the uterus becomes more vascular and glandular, and sexual receptivity is heightened in the female.

Sexual readiness in male bats is synchronized with that of the females and thus occurs once or twice a year for a period of about one or two months each time. The testes enlarge and descend into the scrotum (they are otherwise intra-abdominal) and produce mature spermatozoa. The male then develops a drive to seek out females and to mate.

Bat courtship and mating have rarely been observed in nature. We have, however, observed scattered examples in several genera of bats in captivity. The males come up to the female at their daytime roost and court by emitting certain peculiar purring, buzzing, or chittering sounds which have substantial sonic as well as ultrasonic components. Before mating, male and female gesticulate at each other, with their thumbs, forearms, and wings, and sometimes seem to embrace. Whether the female is in a horizontal position or hanging, the male always makes his approach from the rear. The penis in most bats is unusually long relative to body size, to make it possible to reach around the interfemoral membrane of the female. We do not know how long courtship normally lasts but it seems that no pair bond persists beyond copulation. We do not know whether bats, either males or females, mate more than once during a single season. We also know very little of how males and females find each other during the mating season.

The gestation period of a few bats has been studied. Where known, it is not uncommonly about 16 weeks. For the most part, a single baby is born of each pregnancy, though several genera in North America, including *Eptesicus*, *Lasiurus* and *Lasionycteris*, have multiple births. *Eptesicus fuscus* often bear twins while the lasiurine bats may bear triplets or quadruplets. The greater reproductive rate of these genera presumably reflects greater mortality. As a rule, there is only one birth a year but a number of tropical species are now known to bear young twice a year. About 90 per cent or more of the females of a given population of bats are likely to conceive in each season. Some, of course, miscarry. Firm data on the proportions of live births and survival to adulthood in several species are only now being accumulated.

At birth, infant bats of several genera weigh about 20 per cent of their mother's weight. They have relatively large hind feet and poorly developed wings. Their heads, including the ears, are small (an adaptation for easy delivery) but the mouth itself is large (as in many other mammals).

In giving birth, the mother assumes a hammock-like posture, holding to the cave ceiling or branch with its thumb and toe claws. The infant often appears feet first. In fact, the infant's foot or feet may take hold of a branch, the ceiling, or the mother's leg before its head is clear. The infant usually immediately takes hold of one of its mother's nipples. The position of the functional nipples in bats is usually axillary, under the arm, so that the infant can be covered by its mother's wing while it feeds. There is usually only one nipple and one functional mammary gland on each side. In several families of bats, the females also have "false" nipples in the inguinal region to which the infants cling when not nursing. The mother cleans the embryonic membranes off the baby and generally grooms it but as far as we know does not necessarily sever the umbilical cord or eat the placenta. The placenta may be delivered by the pulling efforts of the infant as it crawls to its mother's breast. Both cord and placenta dry up and drop off after several days.

In many species, the young bat is carried by the mother at all times until shortly before it fledges, i.e. is able to fly, at about six weeks of age. Thus the mother has to fly with a heavy burden, about half her own weight eventually. This is a load which could be disabling if it were off center. The baby is sometimes carried in a position across its mother's chest, like a bandolier, holding the nipple in its mouth and

Two male giant African leaf-nosed bats, *Hipposideros commersoni gigas*, engage in a fierce battle brought on by proximity. The males of this species appear to be unusually intolerant of each other but their ferocity usually ends short of doing physical damage.

with its feet around a leg. If the baby is holding onto a false nipple, it may ride with its legs around its mother's neck. Whatever the position, the young are so hard to see that I have often failed to notice them when I first captured their mothers.

In certain species, including *Erophylla*, *Natalus*, *Chilonatalus*, and *Balantiopteryx*, the young cling to the cave wall and remain behind when the mothers fly out to feed. They sometimes engage in some social activity in the absence of their mothers but are apparently inhibited from doing very much by the dangers of moving on a wall and falling. In Jamaica, I have seen young *Natalus* clinging to older but not quite fledged bats while the mothers were away. In fact, when I first saw them, I thought that the larger bats of the pairs were some new species since they were unlike any adults I had previously come upon. I reasoned that they had to be adults since they were apparently nursing young bats. It took closer inspection to straighten me out.

LIKE PUPPIES OR KITTENS

Among bats which live in crevices, especially free-tailed bats, the young all join together for the greater part of the day or night to play and tussle, stage sham battles and pursuits, and otherwise romp in a fashion which reminds one of a litter of puppies or kittens. In an attic, for example, a group of 30 or 40 youngsters ranging in age from a few days to six weeks or so may gather together while their mothers rest or groom themselves. It has not yet been established whether each mother reclaims its own youngster from these groups. It has been established in the laboratory that the mothers and babies of several species of molossids recognize one another and pair off again after being separated. Their recognition involves audible and ultrasonic vocal signals and probably smell as well. A different pattern is followed by the Mexican free-tailed bats which roost in nursery colonies of several million; their "milk herd" system is described elsewhere.

Young bats roost freely with adult females until they are sexually mature—often one or two years later. They then segregate by sex as do the adults.

All in all, we must conclude that very little has yet been documented on the subject of social behavior in bats. Do they, for example, ever hunt together in a significant fashion? Do they migrate together? What kinds of communication occur among individuals? These are but a few of the many questions which remain to be probed and possibly answered in the future.

HYGIENE

All bats are exceptionally sanitary. On awakening they usually flex their knees and ankles, changing their angle of suspension so that the urinary stream does not soil themselves or their neighbors.

Healthy bats are always clean and fluffy. They spend a substantial portion of the day (and part of the night too) in meticulous grooming. Hanging by one foot, they comb their fur thoroughly with the other foot several times a day, cleaning their toes of the combings with their teeth and lips. Many bats, especially the fruit and nectar feeders, whose pelages are bound to get sticky, also clean their fur with their tongues. Ears and nose leafs often get particular attention. A bat whose pelage is soiled or matted may be considered moribund.

Bats preen their wings almost endlessly. They pass their tongue and lips over the skin of the wings, bit by bit, seemingly softening, moistening, and cleansing simultaneously. They almost surely also spread oils from sebaceous glands over the thin and vulnerable skin of the wing.

Even in hibernation, bats may awaken from time to time to urinate and to groom themselves. In humid caves, droplets of water may condense on their coats and give them a be-jeweled appearance. But because of the healthy condition of the coat, the water remains on the surface of the pelage and the bat itself does not get wet.

The giant free-tailed bat, *Cheiromeles torquata*, is the only one known to have evolved a special accessory for cleansing its skin. These bats are naked except for a few whiskers on the muzzle and a tuft of stiff hairs on the outer lateral surface of the first toe. The tuft is shaped like a brush and with it they assiduously work over their bare skin.

The leaf-nosed bats, *Hipposideros*, usually roost in small groups numbering several dozens, with the individuals adjacent but not touching one another. The extent of separation between bats which roost together but spaced out, varies with species and sex. However, a standard appears to become established and is then reinforced by bickering and sham battles.

ROOSTING PATTERNS

Flying foxes, *Pteropus giganteus*, roost in trees in large groups called camps *(opposite)*. As in this case, there may be sub-clusters consisting of several touching bats separated from nearby groups. What relates the individuals in a cluster to each other is not known. Constant vocal bickering and threatening postures seem to regulate the spacing and sub-grouping but we do not know the causes of the disputes or the sex, age and relationships of the participants.

A PAINFUL "BATTLE"

Here are later stages of the sham battle between the African leaf-nosed bat shown at the opening of this chapter. To make the action clearer for humans accustomed to seeing heads at the top of bodies (and pages), the pictures have been reproduced upside down.

The bats lunge at each other with open mouths and bared fangs, rapidly shifting position with the use of both legs and arms. At the same time they emit loud—perhaps painfully loud—clicks and screeches which are largely ultrasonic. The arms do not appear to be used as weapons but rather for balance or as anchors in gaining a postural advantage over the opponent. Serious wounds are rarely inflicted; instead, one of the participants usually moves away far enough to remove the stimulus for engagement. When confined, however, these bats will often fight until fatal wounds are suffered by one or both.

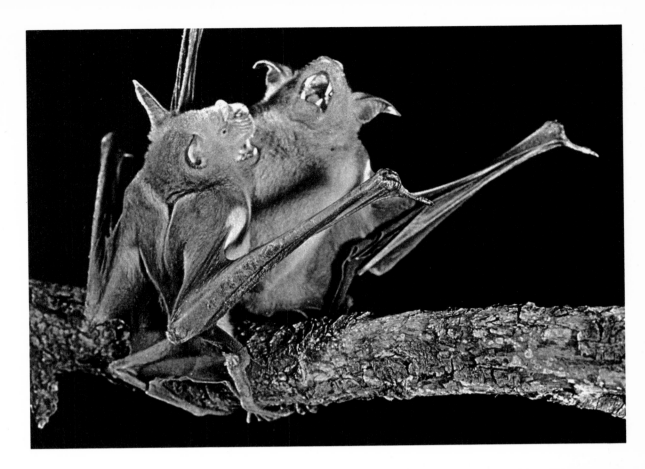

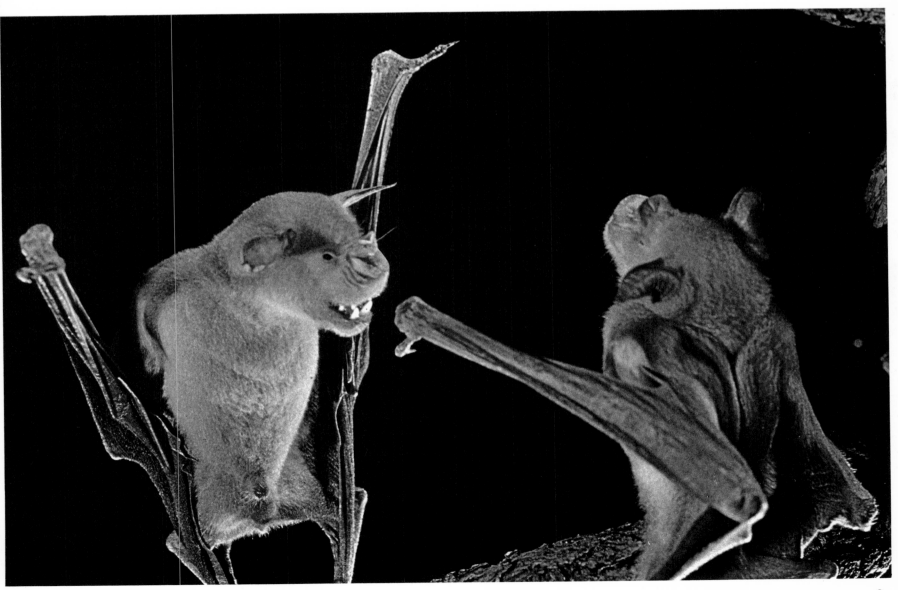

The pictures of these quarreling flying foxes, like those of the preceding African leaf-nosed bats, are reproduced upside down. These bats fight with their thumbs as well as with their teeth. They strike, scratch, and tear with the thumb claw. The group appears to have ganged up against an "outcast."

GROUP AGAINST ONE

The cause of this antagonism between the group and the "outcast," which persisted over a long period, was never discovered. Clearly the fighting was not sham. At right, one of the group bites the object of its joint hostility. The loner died not long afterward, possibly of the wounds he received here.

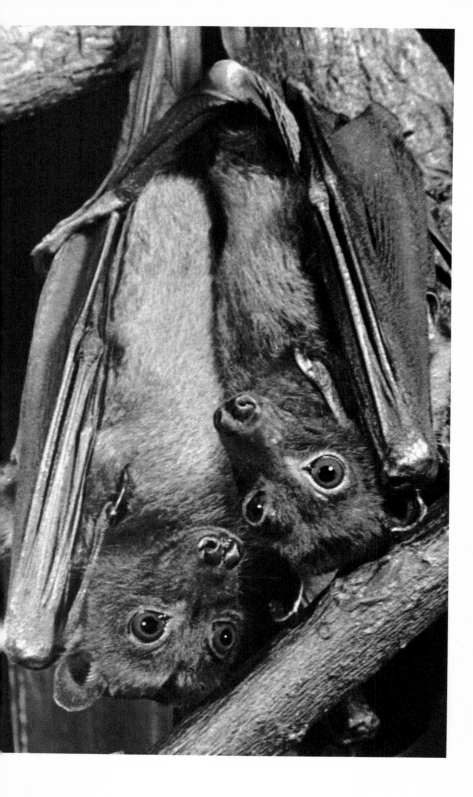

A pair of flying foxes, a male and a pregnant female, hang together while resting at their roost. They appear to be intimate and affectionate, even nuzzling like dogs.

This group of vampires comprises a male and a mother supporting her adolescent child on her back as she rests *(right)*. In this species, as in many others, the close association of a mother with her child often persists for months. In the picture below, the male, apparently alerted by some change in the environment, has moved to a position of readiness to retreat.

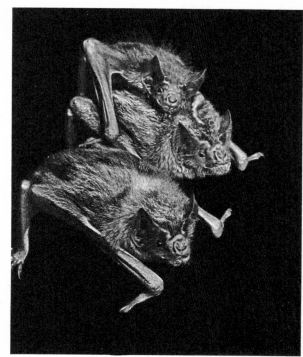

GROUPS AND LONERS

The velvety free-tailed bats, *Molossus rufus nigricans*, generally roost alone in buildings where they press their bodies closely against beams or masonry. Often they emerge before sundown and lie prostate on a rock, as this molossid is doing.

Chilonycteris parnellii, the greater mustache bats, cluster in tight aggregates in their daytime roosts. While isolated individuals of this species invariably seem agitated, in a group they appear to become tranquilized. The greater mustache bats are seen on the opposite page sleeping or resting quietly. On being disturbed *(above)* *Chilonycteris* arch their necks, prop themselves against each other, and search for the source of disturbance by sonar. They emit signals by mouth, forming their lips into the shape of a megaphone.

The least fruit bat, *Artibeus nana*, shown at the right among bananas, roosts either wholly alone or in small groups. In either case it it roosts on or in vegetation.

Just inside the entrance to Bracken Cave the air seems alive with bats
All during the day there is activity, with bats flying about, then settling
down again. When the time approaches for their exit from the cave the
movements assume a more purposeful pattern.

MATERNITY CAVES
OF FREE-TAILED BATS

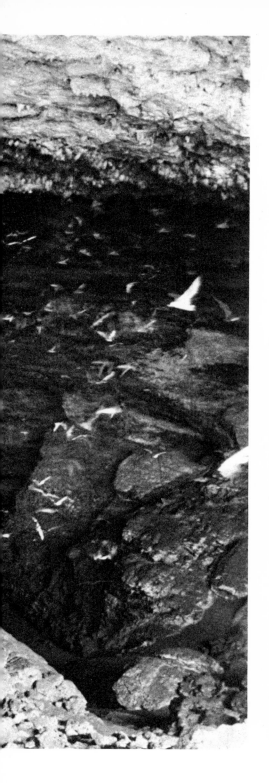

A bat that has just returned to roost on the cave wall is approached by a baby whom she will nurse. The infant is probably not hers; instinct apparently leads the mothers to suckle any of the newborn young of the cave.

On these and the following pages are pictures taken at Bracken Cave near San Antonio, Texas. This is one of a number of caverns where guano, or Mexican free-tailed, bats (*Tadarida brasiliensis mexicana*) come each year to give birth and rear their young. It is estimated that 100 million adult females make the annual migration north from Mexico to the Texas caves. Bracken apparently has the largest single population, estimated at about 20 million adults. The lactating females of these colonies provide an example of the "milk herd" method of feeding the young. The babies are left behind when the adults go out each night to hunt insects. Though each mother has only one offspring, the vast number of infants alone, it is argued, would make it difficult for her to relocate her own child on her return. Instead, each mother, returning to the cave, appears to be prepared to suckle the first or the first two babies that reach her after she lands on the cave wall. We do not at present know whether a mother maintains any relationship at all with her own infant.

A bat has just landed among a group of babies and has immediately attracted their hungry attention. One youngster has already started feeding on her right side *(above)*. The sequence at the right shows two babies feeding while partially covered by the mother's wings. The one on her right pushes at her so aggressively that she is partially turned over. In the photograph on the opposite page two adults can be seen nursing. Blind babies clutch almost every part of the body of the mother at the left. As their coloring reveals, the immature animals shown here are of different ages. Newborn infants are naked and pink. Later, as their dark fur begins to grow they look first bluish, then grey.

THE "MILK HERD" AND THEIR YOUNG

The guano bats, indeed all bats, are tremendous producers of milk. There appear to be two nursing periods each day, and for these each mother provides a quantity of milk equal to nearly one-fourth of her own weight. Milk has occasionally been found in the stomach of some grown-ups in the cave. These may have been individuals who were not able to fly out and feed normally and fed instead on milk obtained from their returning neighbors.

The young are large at birth and grow very rapidly in order to be independent, skilled at hunting, and competent to migrate 1,500 miles by autumn. The babies are adept at clinging to the cave wall. When not nursing, they hang in clusters so tightly packed that if one is picked off the wall, a string of as many as fifteen may come along with it.

When men first came upon the sight of guano bats emerging from their maternity caves in streams of millions, they thought they were seeing smoke billow out of some geologic oddity. The bats begin to emerge in daylight and the exodus continues well into the night. The picture at the left shows the earliest to emerge, just after leaving the entrance of the cave. Earlier many had been milling about in the cave chamber nearest the entrance before they formed up to begin the flight out.

The sun is still shining and is reflected by the bats' wings (below). As this photograph taken near the mouth of the cave shows, seemingly unending swarms of bats continue to emerge into the daylight.

A great number of the first to emerge have now formed into a long, undulating column and are on high flight paths to their insect-hunting grounds. At the same time, new groups, which had probably been roosting in chambers farther back in the cave, are making their appearance *(left)*.

THE GREAT EXODUS

An hour or so before dusk, bats begin to come out of the cave, flying at high speeds. As they form up for the flight, they often collide with one another. Investigators listening carefully in the dark inside the cave have heard the slap of leather on leather as wings clash. The stream of emerging bats has been estimated to contain 200 to 500 individuals per foot of cross section of column, but if their emergence has been delayed, their density may rise to 1,000 individuals per foot. These bats feed on insects at high altitudes and within a radius of 50 miles. Taken together, all of the guano bats of Texas are estimated to consume about 6,600 tons of insects annually.

A giant African leaf-nosed bat, *Hipposideros commersoni gigas*, busies itself with its daily grooming, a task which all bats perform with scrupulous care. First it cleans and moistens the claws of its toes with its tongue and lips after combing its fur, then *(right)* uses the claws to clean its nose leaf.

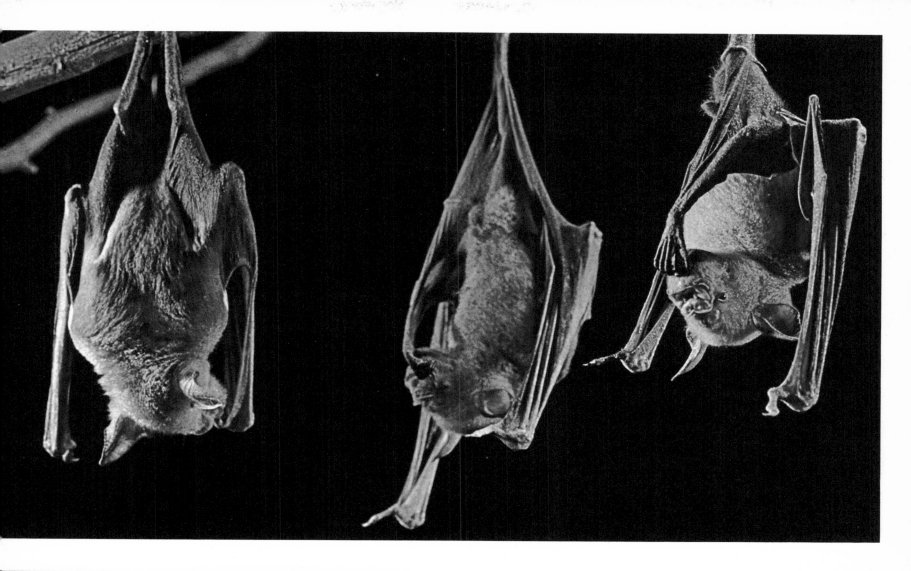

Three *Hipposideros* grooming themselves. The one at the left is going over its wings with its tongue while the other two bats, which have both been combing their fur, are cleaning and moistening their toe-claws.

The mouth of a large dermal gland, which is above the nose leaf in this species, is wide open in the picture at left, whereas previously *(opposite page, top)* the opening was slit-like. The secretions of this gland may be used by the *Hipposideros* in grooming.

The daily toilet of flying foxes. At the right and below a flying fox is at work on the inner surface of its right wing, going through some contortions to get to remote areas.

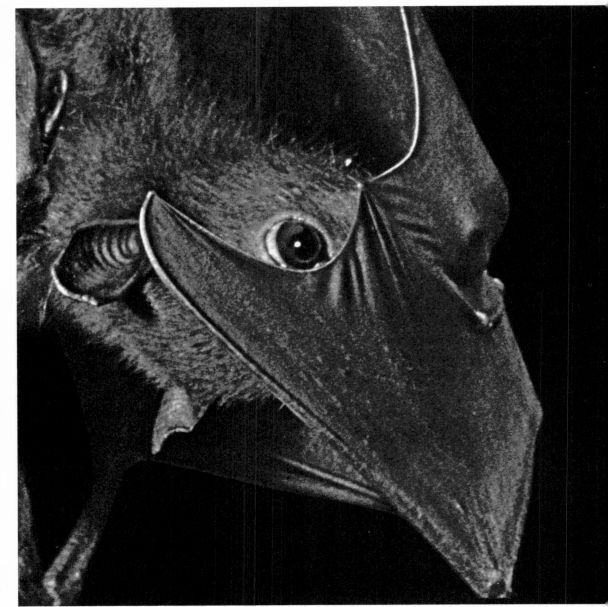

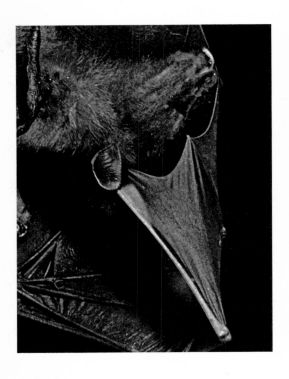

At right, one flying fox helps another groom by lending his tongue for the process of licking a folded wing.

Opposite page: a flying fox twisting in order to groom the lower back with its tongue.

A flying fox uses its left foot to clean an ear. All bats appear to give particular attention to their ears when grooming themselves. Probably this reflects the importance of the ears as sense organs and perhaps their accessibility to and infestation by parasites.

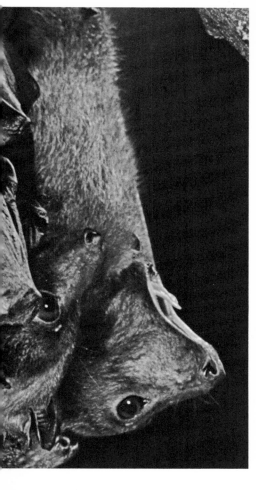
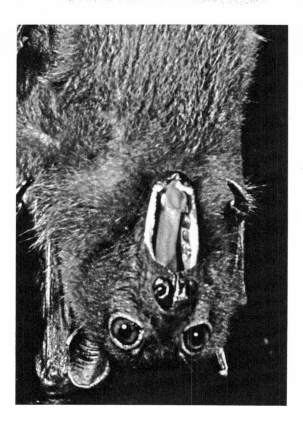

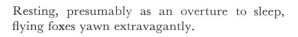
Resting, presumably as an overture to sleep, flying foxes yawn extravagantly.

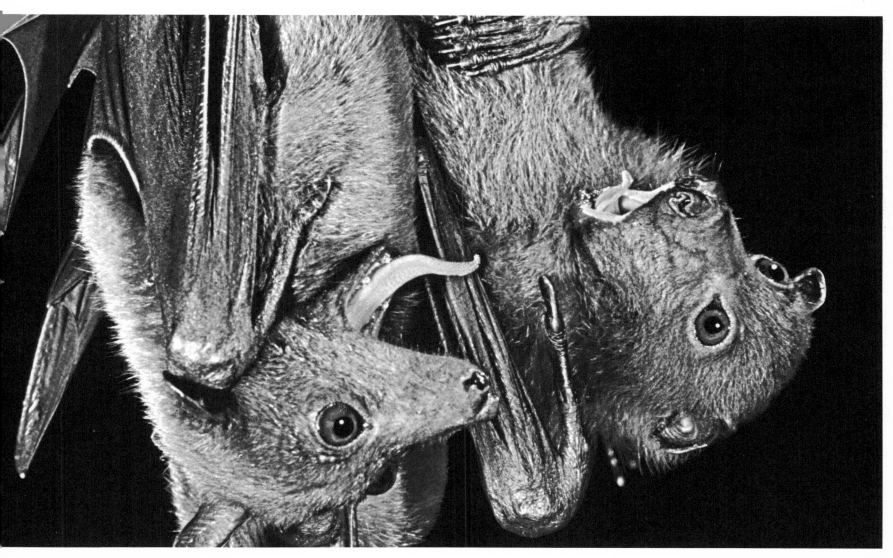

FORAGING

The ancestors of present-day bats, at least of the Microchiroptera, may have lived entirely on insects, and, in general, insects still make up the bulk of bat diets. Bats enjoy an almost exclusive franchise on night-flying insects, whose numbers need not be estimated for anyone who has been outdoors on a summer evening. A few relatively uncommon birds, such as night hawks, and of course web-spinning spiders compete with bats but the numbers they account for are trivial (to the bats if not to the insects).

Insects are highly nutritious. They are the dietary staple of many genera of anteaters and of a variety of other small mammals, birds, lizards, frogs, and fish. There are even insectivorous insects—dragonflies and parasitic wasps among them. Almost all insectivores other than bats, however, hunt either during the day or on the ground or in the water at night. Indeed, nocturnal flight in insects may be an adaptation, in part, to avoid their predators. Why then have so few other insectivores followed bats into the night air? To locate, track, and capture flying prey at night, a predator must have a sensory system that does not require light. The echolocation or sonar system of bats performs this task. Other predatory groups, however, have not yet evolved comparable systems. (Web-spinning spiders filter the air rather than track their prey individually.)

Most bats feed on a variety of insects such as moths, gnats, and beetles. Others seem to have more specialized tastes and more selective hunting techniques. The Malaysian free-tailed bat, *Cheiromeles*, is said to be so selective that it seeks out ants engaged in their nuptial flight. Naturalists have observed that most species of bats have characteristic hunting altitudes and that they normally hunt in a particular kind of terrain that they apparently prefer—over cultivated fields, over water, or under the jungle canopy, for example. Thus different species probably encounter and sample different populations of insects. Bats fragment their prey so effectively before before swallowing them that often only an expert can identify even a portion of the remains from stomach contents. Adequate samples of stomach contents are, in any event, hard to come by. Meaningful analyses are possible only if the bat is taken and examined while actually in the process of feeding or, at the latest, immediately thereafter since their efficiency in fragmenting their food greatly accelerates digestion.

Many bats which prey on large insects have habitual night roosts to which they repair to chew and swallow their catch.

The discarded, often inedible, parts such as wings or legs accumulate in heaps below. Such discard heaps have been collected and analyzed but data from studies of this sort are inadequate: they are prejudiced in favor of bats which have regular night roosts; they exclude parts which have been carried off by scavengers; and they take no account of insects eaten on the wing. All in all, we know too little of who's who in an insectivorous bat's diet.

Recent studies have attempted to assess the quantity of insects which bats consume. In our laboratory, mustache bats, *Chilonycteris*, capture fruit flies at the rate of two per second for short periods and up to 15 or 20 per minute over longer periods. These rates are probably exceeded in nature. Little brown bats, *Myotis*, have been estimated to feed in nature at the rate of 150 large insects or 5,000 very small ones per hour. Some small bats may consume over half their weight in insects per night. Mexican free-tailed bats in Texas have been estimated to consume at least 6,600 tons or 6 million kg of insects per year. Not surprisingly, some insects have learned to fight back. Several families of moths have evolved ears that are sensitive to the ultrasonic frequencies of bat orientation pulses. Some noctuid moths, for example, when they hear a bat at close range (1 meter or so) will take evasive action—fold their wings and plummet to the ground, or fly wild, spiral loops. The bats often seem to be confused by these unpredictable flight patterns and the moths escape.

AN ACOUSTIC WARNING?

When members of another family of moths, the arctiids, hear a bat at close range, they produce a train of ultrasonic clicks. The clicks apparently inhibit bats from capturing arctiids but the mechanism of inhibition is not fully understood. We do know, however, that the arctiid moths are also conspicuously marked and offensively flavored. In many cases, conspicuous markings in animals are believed to have evolved as warnings to predators which hunt by sight, telling them that their potential victim is unpalatable. The clicks may be the acoustic parallel of warning coloration. Their message would be: "Leave me alone. I taste bad."

Insectivorous bats detect and catch their prey by echolocation. The greater mustache bat, *Chilonycteris parnellii*, usually detects a target at a range of about 3.5 meters. Within about

100 milliseconds, the bat has started to alter its own path to intercept that of the insect and, before a second has passed, the bat has usually captured and ingested its prey. The lesser mustache bat, *Chilonycteris psilotis*, has a shorter range, about 0.7 meters, and may complete a capture in as little as a quarter of a second.

Some bats have been shown by high speed photography to capture large insects, always after having located them by sonar, by gathering them in with one wing. When a large insect hits the wing membrane, it is pulled in toward the mouth and grasped by the teeth. The bat then brings its legs and interfemoral membrane forward. Pressing the insect into the membrane, the bat readjusts its hold so as to guide the captive, usually head first, into its mouth. The interfemoral membrane is as a rule particularly well developed in insectivorous bats, especially in those which feed on relatively large creatures.

Most insectivorous bats, immediately upon capturing their prey, disable it by biting into its head. A large insect is usually roughly chewed, initially, and the rather big pieces are temporarily stored in the cheeks. The bat later rechews the stored material at leisure, sometimes in flight, sometimes while roosting. Small insects are probably captured directly by mouth and are often chewed and swallowed immediately. When very abundant, these may also be temporarily stored in the cheeks after being killed.

In captivity, insectivorous bats are usually fed on the larvae of meal beetles, *Tenebrio*, which go under the name of meal worms or golden grubs. These are easily raised in large numbers at low cost and are simple to confine, pleasant to handle, and appetizing to bats. Almost all bats must be hand-fed at the outset but, once introduced to meal worms, many learn to find their food in dishes. Some species of bats will eat the adult beetles or the pupae, but most will not. The adults have a strong odor which may be offensive to bats. I believe that the beetles also have an unpalatable flavor which has probably evolved as a defense mechanism. All bats which adapt to captivity will eat the larvae but many will eat only the anterior portion of each meal worm, regularly ejecting the remainder. Others eat only the gut or the fat body, but these, almost surely malnourished after a day or two of such pickiness, do not survive in captivity.

Many insects are unpalatable to insectivorous animals, including bats. Not all defenses, however, work equally well against all bats. In captivity, bats usually refuse to eat the common American cockroach, which emits an offensive odor when disturbed. But in our laboratory, *Antrozous* and *Macrotus* have fed themselves almost exclusively (one *Macrotus* for five years) on roaches that they captured themselves in their flight chamber. When feeding *Macrotus* in the field, I have also discovered that if a mixed bag of moths captured around a light in the evening is placed in the bats' cage, by morning all of the inconspicuously colored individuals but none of the brightly patterned ones would be consumed.

A GRASSHOPPER OR GNATS?

Several genera of bats have specialized for capturing terrestrial arthropods such as insects, spiders, and scorpions on the ground, on walls, or on vegetation. For several reasons their task would seem to be harder than that of the bats which catch insects in flight. First, the prey must be hard to locate among the irregularities of ground cover or bark. Second, landing would often be required for catches of this sort, but bats in general are poorly adapted for landing on and taking off from some of these surfaces; many species also walk poorly. On the other hand there are compensations. Many of the arthropods that these bats seek are large; one of them alone might make a meal. A single grasshopper, locust, cricket, roach, praying mantis, or scorpion could make up a large fraction of a bat's daily caloric requirement. Considering the cost, in energy, of tracking individual insects, the advantage to be gained by replacing 5,000 gnats with one large grasshopper might be considerable.

In any event, some bats do feed in this way and do so very effectively. These include *Macrotus*, *Plecotus*, *Antrozous*, and probably *Euderma* among those shown here. Under difficult detection conditions, I believe these bats locate their prey by their ventilation or antennal movements or by locomotor actions if any occur. (All insects move slightly in order to ventilate their tracheal respiratory system.) These bats also all hover well, have exceedingly large ears, and use a low intensity sonar output—features which are undoubtedly associated with their hunting habits. The full story of their way of life, however, remains to be assembled.

Several species of bats have turned to feeding on vertebrates such as tree-frogs, small lizards, birds, mice, shrews, and small bats. Two carnivorous bats of this kind are the so-called false vampires of the Old World, *Megaderma lyra* of India and Ceylon and *Macroderma gigas* of Australia. Both also feed on large insects at times. Members of a closely related species, *Megaderma spasma*, feed on large insects that rest on the ground or on walls but never on vertebrates. It seems reasonable to suppose, therefore, that the carnivorous species, using ancestral hunting and capturing techniques, have simply switched from large invertebrates to small vertebrates.

Why have not more bats made a similar switch to exploit the abundance of small vertebrates in the tropics? Perhaps bat size and predatory skill are both limitations. Few bats are large enough to prey on vertebrates. In particular, few insectivorous bats are large, though there is at least one of striking size in most families. It might be thought that vertebrates can defend themselves better than invertebrates. But do they do so? Small bats, small birds asleep, tree-frogs, lizards—these are not formidable enemies. I have watched *Megaderma lyra* prey on small horseshoe bats in a large cage. The predators pounce on their victims, engulfing their prey with their very wide wings, probably to preclude escape. Shortly afterwards, it can be seen that the dead bat has had the back of its skull crushed or its neck broken by a powerful bite. Apparently *Megaderma* "know" that prey with serious central nervous system injuries are helpless. This kind of predatory skill and awareness plus the ability to select "easy" prey may be the requisites for success as carnivores.

The other known carnivorous bats are the large Neotropical false vampires and their relatives, including *Vampyrum spectrum* (shown in this chapter), *Chrotopterus*, and *Phyllostomus hastatus* of the family Phyllostomatidae. Some of these eat fruit and even insects in captivity as well as meat and small vertebrates. They almost surely eat fruit in the wild as well. Their non-carnivorous relatives of the subfamily Phyllostomatinae are either insectivorous (*Macrotus*, for example), or frugivorous. These spear-nosed carnivorous species are very large bats with smallish ears; among their closest non-carnivorous relatives is a small frugivorous species of *Phyllostomus*. These points, insubstantial though they are, all support the hypothesis of frugivorous ancestry for these carnivores.

The transition from fruit to vertebrates may seem more abrupt than that from insects to vertebrates. Viewed in terms of locating and taking prey, however, the difference may not be so great. Small sleeping vertebrates are probably not usually

as fragrant as fruit, which bats probably seek out by scent, bu they are often found in trees and they are bulky and relatively immobile. Many bat fruits (and flowers), in addition, ar produced directly from wood, the stem coming directly from the trunk or from a branch. If such a position for fruit or flowers facilitates a bat's approach, are not roosting birds or lizards resting on trees also vulnerable?

The carnivorous bats belong to two families noted for hovering flight and for poor ambulatory locomotion. Hovering is probably essential for adequate lift to make take-offs with heavy loads, for these bats often carry their prey to habitua roosts for consumption. Sometimes they, like insectivorous bats discard some parts—feet, wings, tail—which pile up below their roosts.

In two other families, several species have specialized for catching and eating fish and small crustaceans. In both families, the fish-eaters, *Noctilio leporinus* of the family Nocti lionidae, and *Pisonyx* and two species of *Myotis* of the family Vespertilionidae can barely be distinguished, even by experts from their insectivorous relatives. The only obvious and uniform distinction is that the fishing forms have enormou hind feet and claws. The transition from the pursuit o insects to gaffing fish is difficult to reconstruct. *Noctilio leporinu* often also pursue insects successfully and sometimes apparentl subsist on insects alone. Less is known of the dietary and fishing habits of the others. *Noctilio* is shown in this chapte and is discussed in greater detail below.

All of the fishing bats are found on oceanic shores: *Noctili* around much of the Caribbean and along other Neotropica shores and inland as well (roosting in small caves and hollow trees), *Pisonyx* in Baja California (roosting under rocks or ir boulder heaps), and *Myotis macrotarsus* in the Philippines (roos ting in tidal caves). *Noctilio* are known to fish in both fresh and salt water but *Pisonyx* and *Myotis* may exploit only the latter

Is it significant that the fishers walk well? Perhaps relativel well-developed leg musculature is required for fishing. Perhap leg injuries may be encountered in fishing and a bat that car walk and crawl (into crevices, for example) is therefore mor apt to survive than one which must rest by hanging suspended from overhead surfaces. A remarkable number of small but intriguing speculations can be generated about almost ever aspects of this subject. Comprehensive scientific investigation may someday provide answers to some of these questions—and will probably at the same time reveal new ones.

FRUIT EATERS AND ECOLOGY

Many genera of two families of bats feed on fruit. All of the Megachiroptera do, at least part of the time. In the New World tropics, over thirty genera of spear-nosed bats, the Phyllostomatidae, feed on a wide variety of wild fruit and berries. Not all favor the same fruits. In Panama, for example, the beautiful tent-building bat, *Uroderma*, feeds voraciously on a small, hard, green fruit which is a relative of the cashew. The ground under *Uroderma* roosts is deeply littered with the large seeds of this fruit interlaced with a thicket of sprouting seedlings. (Ghostly seedling groves are also common sights in caves inhabited by fruit-eating bats. Each bat usually carries home a piece of fruit to chew on; the dropped seeds sprout. In the absence of light the seedlings are etiolated—ghostly in color and lacking formed foliage.)

Frugivorous bats usually chew the fruit thoroughly and swallow the juice and mushy portion while spitting out the pulp and seeds. This procedure allows them to ingest nutritious material without adding unnecessary weight—a real concern for an animal which has to expend a significant amount of energy to carry each gram in flight. But this procedure has also been exploited evolutionarily by many kinds of tropical plants which often produce fruit with large, hard, unpalatable seeds that are easily cleaned and dropped by bats or fruit with exceptionally slippery seeds which pop out of the bat's mouth as it chews. Thorough fragmentation by the bat speeds digestion and also saves weight and energy. Frugivorous bats may start eliminating the remains of a meal in 30 minutes to an hour after having started to feed. This rapid digestion also appears to preclude the support of a large bacterial flora in the digestive tract, thus again saving weight.

Since many fruits have a short ripening season, frugivorous bats must vary their diet throughout the year or migrate, as several genera do. Their migrations may well be determined by seasonal ripening of wild crops but there may be other considerations, such as seasonal variations in weather.

In captivity in temperate climates, most frugivorous bats will eat all types of melon but usually refuse other local fruits. They will avidly consume bananas, mangoes, papayas, guavas, and some other tropical fruits when these are available. Some genera—flying foxes and *Lissonycteris*, for example—have much more catholic tastes and will accept many more varieties of fruit, including citrus and pineapple.

A curious fact about most frugivorous bats in my experience is that they cannot or will not open or peel their own bananas, mangoes, or melons in captivity. I believe this to be true of most of them in nature, too. How then do they eat? I have seen *Rousettus* bite through green banana skins but never through ripe skins. Perhaps banana skins, and those of some other fruits, develop a deterrent taste as they ripen in order to discourage marauding mammals. In Panama I have observed large numbers of ripe cultivated mangoes being opened each day by flocks of parakeets and being left partly eaten. These mangoes are consumed during the next night by bats. Wild mangoes are much smaller—they are said to be "designed" for bats. Perhaps cultivation has selected mango features which protect the fruit from predation. Insects may also open some fruits, unwittingly, for bats. Yet other fruits become accessible when they fall to the ground and break open. Finally, many wild fruits are eaten skin and all.

A leading authority on the ecology of tropical fruits and flowers, Professor L. van der Pijl of the University of Indonesia, believes that large numbers of plants have evolved specifically to have their seeds dispersed by bats. These plants usually bear small green or brown fruit, often with a musky, sour, or rancid odor. Indeed, he points out, the bulk of market fruits in the tropics are unattractive in color and odor while those in temperate regions (often designed to be attractive to birds or other vision-oriented animals) are attractively red, orange, or yellow and have pleasing, fruity fragrances.

THE MIGRATIONS OF FLOWER FEEDERS

Almost all of the Megachiroptera feed on flowers to some extent but one subfamily, the Macroglossinae, feeds principally on pollen, nectar, and petals. Among the spear-nosed bats, two subfamilies, the Glossophaginae and the Phyllonycterinae, are substantially pollen and nectar feeders. The members of all three groups share certain characteristics. They are small, they can hover and fly slowly, and they have elongated snouts and tongues. In many, the tongue is tipped with a brush of dermal papillae which is assumed to be useful in lapping up pollen and nectar. Most feed on fruit as well as flowers and some are known to take insects as well. It has not been established, however, whether insects are taken actively or are ingested inadvertently with the flowers or fruit being eaten. Possibly insects are deliberately sought out because their protein and mineral content are necessary during growth, pregnancy, or lactation.

Flower feeders often migrate seasonally, probably following the blooming seasons of important dietary staples. I have visited a cave near Tuxtla Gutierrez in Mexico, for example, in midsummer and found it inhabited by about 500,000 *Leptonycteris*. Other biologists report never having seen a single *Leptonycteris* there at any other time of year.

Perhaps the most extraordinary diet among bats is that of the vampires. These three genera of New World tropical bats feed exclusively on blood. *Desmodus*, the common vampire, takes blood chiefly from livestock and large wild mammals such as deer and peccaries. *Diaemus* and *Diphylla* prefer bird blood—principally from chickens and other large domestic fowl nowadays, but in the past surely from many large, wild species.

Adult vampires, in good physical condition, weigh about 30 grams (one ounce). Their nightly intake, in captivity, is about 16 ccs (one tablespoon) of blood. In nature, they probably consume a little more than that because of the additional energy they expend in hunting for their prey. Vampire bites *per se* are not serious. The wound is clean and the amount of blood lost is insignificant to a large mammal. (Whether the blood loss is equally insignificant to a chicken has not been established. Since fowl are always more common than large mammals, however, one would expect the same bird not to be molested very often.) Unfortunately, however, bot flies abound in many tropical countries and they lay their eggs in broken skin, including the wounds left by vampires. The bot fly larvae burrow into the flesh and develop there as parasites which, being painful and irritating, often affect the host's rest and appetite. Vampires are also known to be vectors of rabies (as, indeed, are almost all mammals) and of a trypanosomiasis (an infestation by a parasitic organism) that affects cattle.

Vampires domesticate more readily than most bats. They not only take to being handled after a few days, but most individuals also come to accept defibrinated blood collected at a slaughter house, refrigerated, and served in a dish. As far as we know, they never eat any other food.

Evolutionarily, vampires are clearly derived from advanced, frugivorous, spear-nosed bats. The intermediate stages are not known, but finding fruit and finding large animals or birds in

the jungle probably require much the same techniques, and perhaps biting into plant and animal skins and feeding on the juices may also be similar acts.

VAMPIRES AND HUMANS

Vampires rarely bite men. I have often inquired about this. In most parts of Mexico, country people in regions where cattle are regularly bitten by vampires have looked at me with incredulity and have patronizingly replied that vampires bite animals, not men. This is not entirely true. They do occasionally bite men but among those who live close to vampires this is considered a rarity.

Some years ago, the distinguished ethologist, Konrad Lorenz, visited our laboratory at a time when we were studying vampires. When he heard that none of us had ever been bitten by a vampire, he replied that he would like to experience such a bite himself. After failing to discourage him, I suggested that he corner and prod one of the bats in order to provoke it. Try as he would, he could induce no more than some angry cries and a great many scrambling escape attempts. I have since been bitten in anger by a newly captured vampire, but as far as I know, Dr. Lorenz has not yet shared the experience.

Vampires are believed to have an anticoagulant enzyme in their saliva though no modern studies have been done on this subject. We know that they repeatedly lick the skin where they intend to bite. This could be an effective way of applying an anticoagulant. Or it could be a method of testing the alertness of their prey; vampires are very timid and quickly withdraw if their intended victim stirs or reacts. A wild and unjustified speculation would be that the bat is engaged in anesthetizing the spot which it intends to bite, for men who *have* been fed upon by vampires in their sleep are not awakened.

A student of mine kept three very domesticated vampires at home in his bedroom one summer while studying their acoustic perception. He reported that one of the bats three times tried to feed upon him. Each time, while the student was quietly reading at his desk, the bat landed on the floor, approached very slowly, taking some minutes to do so, and proceeded to lick his intended victim's foot. Unfortunately the student was wearing moccasins and nothing happened. My pleas that next time he read barefoot were to no avail.

NECTAR FEEDERS AND FLOWER POLLINATORS

The flowers of the saguaro, a tree-like cactus, provide sustenance for *Leptonycteris*. The saguaro is one of a large number of plants adapted for pollination by bats. In these plants the flowers, opening at night, are usually white or inconspicuous, and often project upward beyond the spines or the foliage of a plant. Sometimes they hang at the end of pendulous branches. Other bat-pollinated flowers bloom directly on the wood, isolated from the foliage. They are thus readily accessible to nectar feeders. The saguaro's flowers are exposed beyond the spines of the cactus, so the bats, in addition to feeding from them, can also rest by hanging from them, apparently without suffering injury from the spines. Thus the bats can drink their full, then rest before resuming. One can be seen hanging at right.

Bat-pollinated flowers have been known to produce as much as 7 to 15 ml (0.5 to 1 tablespoon) of nectar, which consists mostly of simple sugars and water. Digestion of the simple sugars in nectar is almost as rapid as the absorption of water, so a meal may perhaps be fully absorbed in thirty minutes, and the bat be ready for another. Pollen is rich in proteins and minerals. Proteins are more slowly digested than the sugars, but are nutritionally necessary.

The sequence of pictures beginning at the left and continuing across the top of these pages shows an impatient nectar feeder forcing open a saguaro flower by ramming its snout into the corolla.

The belly of this *Leptonycteris* almost looks as if it were keeping the bat from plunging deeper into the flower from which it is still feeding. Bats take in food voraciously and will eat until their bellies are almost spherical.

Here *Leptonycteris* display a variety of attack postures while feeding. Though the flowers of the seguaro cactus usually close after a single night, their attraction for bats is so great that pollination is practically ensured. At right, two bats hover over a flower while expertly using their elongate tongues to extract sustenance from the corolla. All nectar feeding bats are endowed with a long, extensible tongue. Sometimes one-quarter the length of the animal, the tongue usually has a soft brush of papillae at its tip. Bat-pollinated flowers not only produce sufficient pollen to nourish the bats but have enough left to pollinate other flowers. They often have a very large number of anthers (the pollen-bearing organs) and bats feeding on them may be literally covered with pollen grains. A number of distinguished mammologists and naturalists, some of them even authorities on bats, have believed temporarily that they had discovered new species when, by chance, they collected yellow bats which had just finished feeding. To their surprise the yellow color dusted off: it was pollen. A modest dusting of grains is visible on the face of one of the bats shown in the photographs overleaf.

The agave plant, a member of the amaryllis family, attracts nectar feeders with deep, projecting flowers. Many nectar feeders migrate according to the season. The *Leptonycteris* shown here move from Mexico into Arizona for the summer. During this time they may feed on fruit as well as flowers.

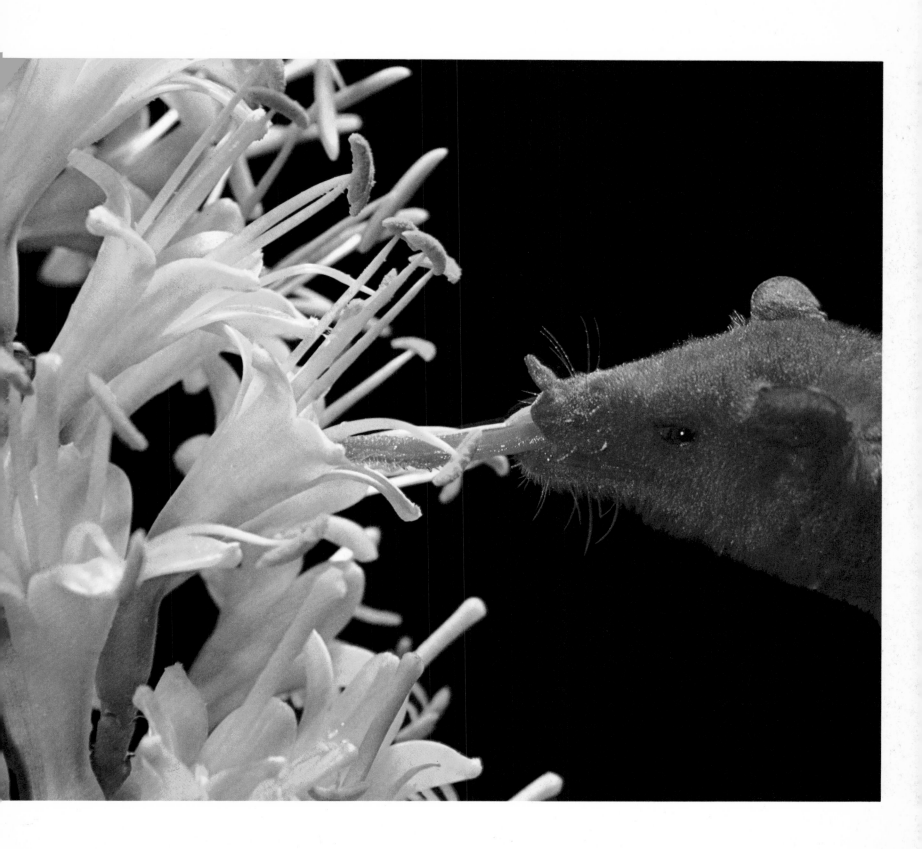

AN "EXTINCT" FLOWER BAT

The pictures on these pages are of the Jamaican flower bat, *Phyllonycteris aphylla*, long believed to be extinct. The diet of flower bats has not been established but in captivity they eat sparingly of some tropical fruits and fruit juices.

Attracted by the smell of a ripe mango broken open by a fall, the bat descends from a branch and settles on the ground with its wings folded. Because it cannot break the skin of such a large fruit, it must search for a place that has been injured, or a part that has been broken into and partially eaten by insects of by a bird. The remarkably long legs and the large feet seem to be particularly adapted for climbing along branches. As far as in known, *Phyllonycteris aphylla* cannot hover, so it may be necessary for them to land on or near their food and to feed by twisting around and engaging in acrobatics.

Here are two pictures of a night-flying silk moth, *Antherea polyphemus*, perhaps taking evasive action by falling backwards when a California leaf-nosed bat, *Macrotus waterhouse californicus*, flies at it. This insectivorous bat uses echolocation to search out prey. When *Macrotus* catch a large moth, they may engulf it with one wing, and often with their interfemoral membrane, before crushing its head. They usually discard the wings, parts of the legs and sometimes the abdomen as well.

BAT VS. MOTH

Some moths have ultrasonic detection mechanisms which enable them to hear the echolocation cries of a bat as far as thirty meters away. At such a distance the moth flies swiftly and directly away from its enemy. When a bat is detected at close range, the moth either begins to fly an erratic path, fold its wings and fall, or power dive to the ground or into vegetation. This sequence of pictures shows an *Antherea polyphemus* dropping after apparently being discovered by a *Macrotus*. These moths, however, are not known to be able to hear, though further studies may show that they do possess this ability. The response of this moth and others seems clear, but the modality has not been established.

BLOOD DRINKER

The common vampire, *Desmodus rotundus*, has the most specialized teeth of any bat. There are two upper incisors (clearly shown in the photograph below), four small lower incisors, two upper and two lower canines and a total of ten cheek teeth. Apparently only the incisors are used in biting a victim. The bites are superficial but the wounds bleed freely from capillaries. The canines are used for biting in defense. No function is known for the additional teeth since the vampire diet is confined to blood. While feeding, a vampire extends its tongue and curls the edges under so as to form a tube with an open ventral "seam" *(left)*. The open side is held against the midline cleft in the lower lip. As the bat feeds, the muscles of the tongue contract visibly and rapidly in a manner that resembles peristalsis. The blood seems to be propelled up into the mouth by these contractions and by capillary action.

CARNIVORE

The pallid bats, *Antrozous pallidus*, range throughout much of western North America, including desert areas. They eat flying insects but will also land to take terrestrial arthropods such as crickets, grasshoppers, beetles and scorpions. Scorpions produce a venom which they use defensively, injecting it into an enemy by means of a stinger located at the end of the abdomen. This venom is dangerous to man; to an animal the size of the pallid bat it should be a serious threat if not lethal. Nevertheless, as the pictures on the following pages show, these bats attack scorpions in dramatic encounters. Whether they are immune to the venom or gain victory by superior tactics has not been established. It seems most likely that they are skilled in disabling their prey while avoiding the scorpion's rather stereotyped defensive movements.

Beginning its attack, a pallid bat menacingly walks toward the scorpion with wings outstretched and its mouth open. As the bat attempts to seize the scorpion *(below)*, the latter raises its stinger.

The scorpion has seized the edge of the bat's wing with one pincer. In an attempt to free itself the bat has raised its wing, carrying the scorpion with it *(left)*. Below, the bat, having shaken free, moves in for the kill while the victim's "tail" beats about, stirring up the soil but not harming its antagonist.

At left, a fishing bat flies over the water uttering its ultrasonic orientation pulses. Then it flies down to the surface and rakes the water with its exceptionally large, well-spread claws and gaffs a fish *(bottom)*.

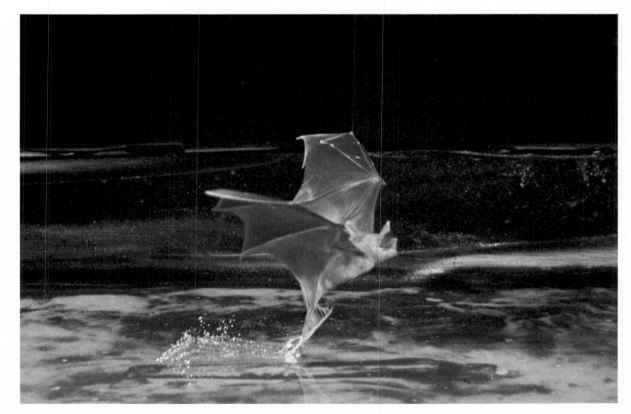

FISHER IN FRESH AND SALT WATER

Noctilio leporinus, the fishing bulldog bats, range from Mexico southward. *Noctilio* are known to orient by echolocation but the role of their echolocation in detecting and tracking fish is still somewhat unclear. Echolocation signals, or any other airborne sounds, are almost completely (99.9%) deflected by the surface of a body of water. In addition, fish, except for their swim bladders which may be filled with air, are close in acoustical values to the water and therefore reflect sound poorly. Recent studies by R. A. Suthers in Trinidad have shown that *Noctilio* in the laboratory can detect tiny wires, one millimeter in diameter and projecting 5 mm through the surface of the water, but cannot detect pieces of fish which have been anchored just beneath the surface on similar wires. It would seem therefore that *Noctilio* echolocate fish when they break or distort the surface. But since these bats often fish successfully in the ocean or in bays where the surface is seemingly perpetually broken, we must admit to not yet fully understanding their methods.

Now flying upward, the bat swiftly brings up the foot which has gaffed the fish in order to transfer the prize to its mouth. *Noctilio* have unusually wide and long wings in relation to their body size, presumably for the lift required to fly with a heavy load.

Having brought the fish up to its mouth, *Noctilio* grasps it with its teeth. By flexing its legs and tail to bring the interfemoral membrane forward and then pressing the fish back against it, *Noctilio* can adjust its mouth-hold as required.

If far from its roost, *Noctilio* may chop up a captured fish roughly and store the pieces in its cheeks, saving final mastication for later. Since these bats send their orientation pulses out by mouth, a mouth-held fish might be thought to interfere with the process. But the picture at top right shows that part of the mouth is clear, so the channel for emission is not blocked.

Overleaf: The Neotropical false vampire *(Vampyrum spectrum)* flies off with a captured mouse. Mice or other small vertebrates are killed or disabled when these bats crush the skull or cervical spine with their powerful bite. With a wing span of about two feet (60 cm) or more, these are the largest bats in the New World. The photograph is life size.

With a roughly chopped-up fish stored in its cheeks, the bat returns to its fishing, flying down to the surface of the water with the outsized toe-claws at the ready for the next gaffing.

LOCOMOTION
AND REPOSE

For all bats, flight is of course the most characteristic mode of locomotion. When they roost during the day, however, or at night, when some land to feed, they may use a variety of other types of movement.

Many species are severely limited in non-flight action: they can do little more than hang by their toe-claws from a cave ceiling, a branch, or a similar overhead surface. Their ambulatory behavior may be no more elaborate than releasing their hold with one foot, reaching out and taking a new hold, and then swinging over. They can swing—upside down—across a ceiling or along a limb if they find adequate toeholds, but may be completely unable to walk on the ground, horizontal surfaces, or on walls. They fly into or up to their roosts, flip over in flight, grasp toeholds, and hang until they are again ready to take flight. Among the bats shown in this book, *Macrotus*, *Leptonycteris*, *Hipposideros*, and *Monophyllus* belong to this category.

Cynopterus, *Pteropus*, and *Rousettus* also are unable to walk in the usual sense but they are adept at climbing along tree limbs. In doing so they use their thumbs as well as their toes, assuming a sloth- or hammock-like posture similar to the position of females when delivering their young.

Some bats, especially the emballonurids, are specifically adapted for roosting on vertical surfaces such as tree trunks or belfry walls. They usually hang suspended by their toes, with their chest and wrists propped against the wall. Others, usually Megachiroptera, hang with feet twisted through 180°. Many wall-roosting species, among other types, can climb backwards up vertical surfaces, sometimes very agilely, reaching foot over foot for new holds. The large flying foxes may climb trees in this fashion but, on occasion, go up head first by using their thumbs. They may do this when they accidentally fall to the ground, being apparently too heavy and poorly adapted for taking off directly from horizontal surfaces or through underbrush.

While many bats of course roost upside down, it is a curious fact that bats of the suborder Microchiroptera hold their head upright when they are alert. The bat fully extends or dorsiflexes the head on the neck so that its ears and facial features are in the same orientation relative to the ground as they would be if the bat were upright. When asleep, these bats may tuck the chin down against the chest, in which case the head is truly upside down.

In the Megachiroptera the head is almost always upside down at the roost. Only when the bat is about to take off does it usually swing over.

The difference between the two groups would appear to be the need for a standard orientation of the ears (relative perhaps to gravity) in evaluating sonar information. The evaluation of visual images, on the other hand, appears to be independent of orientation. Thus the Megachiroptera may hang with the back against a wall or tree trunk. But since this is a position which precludes an upright head posture it is one which never assumed by the Microchiroptera.

THE GOOD WALKERS

A number of families of bats, including the vampires, the mustache, the free-tailed, and the common bats are good walkers. When at rest or walking they hold their wings tightly folded so that the wing membranes and the fingers are out of the way and protected from injury. In one Malaysian free-tailed bat *(Cheiromeles)*, most of the hand portion of the wing is tucked into a pocket formed on each side between the very thick skin of the base of the wing and the back. Their knuckles can be seen bulging through the skin near the spine. Walking bats use their wrists for bearing weight the way other quadrupedal mammals use the palms of their hands or the digits. Some bats also use the thumb and its claw as a walking aid. Many that have particularly well developed legs also have specialized pads on their wrists and soles to improve their grip on vertical or slippery surfaces. (All bats' knees face backwards, almost opposite to the direction of our own, while the toes, which can be moved independently of each other, usually point either backwards or to the side.)

Most walkers roost in caves, boulder heaps, or hollow trees where they often walk or creep into narrow spaces. Certain species are known to crawl back as far as 6 meters or more into crevices in cave walls or in cliffs. There are also bats of this group that have evolved to exploit cracks or secluded spaces in vegetation. In the Philippines and Indonesia, for example, tiny bats *(Tylonycteris)* live in the hollow center of growing bamboo shoots which they enter through cracks which form as the wind bends the bamboo back and forth. In the American tropics, *Thyroptera* dwell inside young leaves which have not yet unfurled. The hoary bats and their relatives often roost on tree trunks, partly tucked behind pieces of projecting bark. Free-tailed bats frequently exploit crevices in buildings as daytime roosts. They utilize all sorts of spaces: between pieces of masonry, among beams, between roofing materials and in the cores of walls and window frames. In the tropics, many free-tailed bat species have undoubtedly become some thousands or millions of times more abundant since the advent of man because of the vastly increased number of suitable roosts his buildings have provided.

Tadarida molossa, which I have captured in Jamaica, live in this way. A colony of about 30 occupied a church steeple 15 to 30 meters above ground. The bats regularly roosted during the day behind one or another of the four brass faces of the steeple clock. The clock faces, perhaps a meter in diameter, were mounted 3 or 4 centimeters out from the vertical stone walls. The bats clung to the stone in seemingly random orientation, shaded but fully exposed to the radiated heat of the sun. They seemed to shift their location from one face of the clock to another as the day wore on, apparently seeking the "sunny exposure." They invariably choose elevated and unobstructed roosts, presumably because their heavy bodies and long narrow wings require that they drop from their perch and gain considerable velocity before they can sustain themselves in flight.

All bats' claws are well curved, sharp and can engage amazingly slight irregularities. Indeed, their hold is often so stable that the bat may not only sleep securely but may even remain in position after death. I have seen bats hang serenely on the fine cracks between carefully fitted sheets of plywood that make up the ceiling of my laboratory as well as from the pitted surface of painted concrete blocks. A cup hook is a gross object in their roosting world.

CHAMPIONS OF AGILITY

The champions of agility are the vampires. They can walk, scurry, tiptoe, leap and fly with a repertory not equaled, in my experience, by any other animal. The length of their forearms and upper arms, the strength and set of their hind legs, and the unusual development of their wrists and thumbs—all these factors allow them to execute a remarkable variety of movements gracefully and smoothly.

Vampires live in crevices in rocks, caves, and hollow trees. In caves, though they may hang from the open ceiling, vampires prefer relatively narrow or partly enclosed side passages or chambers. In tight places of this sort flight is often impossible and so vampires resort to other forms of locomotion—i.e., crawling, walking or leaping. Vampires also resort to jumping to escape from interlopers, and jumping is an advantage in dodging a dangerous defensive action on the part of an intended victim.

Non-walking bats, especially those roosting outdoors, and thus exposed to the weather, partly or completely cover their belly and chest with their wings while at rest. When walkers roost, however, they usually keep their wings tightly folded at their sides. Bats that hang in tight, touching clusters, whether they walk or not, usually keep their wings well folded along their sides; those that hang well-spaced out often enfold their body. The wing posture of roosting bats is probably determined by two considerations: the need to protect themselves against weather and the need to avoid wing injuries which might be inflicted by their fellows. The position of the wings in roosting may also interact with the regulation of body temperature, and temperature regulation may in turn determine to some extent the mode of roosting.

DEAD LEAF? RIPE FRUIT?

Many outdoor roosting bats, such as the flying foxes or their small African relatives, the epaulette bats, *Epomophorus*, are exceptionally well camouflaged when at rest. Their wing-enfolded body, suspended by one leg, and often tinted in shades of gold, orange, or red, resembles a dead leaf or a ripe fruit. The resemblance may be strengthened by the array of similar bats in the same posture repeating the pattern along one or more branches.

Color additionally enhances the cryptic appearance of many bats. The shading is usually darker toward the tail and lighter toward the shoulders, neck, and head. Viewed from above against the dark jungle floor, when the bats are in their normal roosting position, they show dark against dark; viewed from below against the sky, they show bright against bright. Similar designs of countershading are widely recognized among other animals. In addition, many bats which roost in the open have conspicuous flecks or patches of white or bright yellow around their ears or on their shoulders. These might seem to be conspicuous but when seen from below they echo the pattern of bright patches of sunlight or of sky seen through the generally dark jungle canopy.

A colony of the epaulette bats mentioned above often provided me with entertainment when I lunched at a sidewalk cafe in the small town of Uvira on the shore of Lake Tanganyika during a field trip some years ago. They roosted in nearby trees, where they were at first difficult to discern by sight. Their presence would be revealed in time by their beautiful bell-like calls, the function of which is not yet known. (They are also revealed by the accumulation of guano beneath the trees in which they roost.) Once having discovered them I often climbed the very accessible trees to try to capture one or more. The bats looked very somnolent until I was an arm's length away but always suddenly took off before they could be grabbed.

BATS AND WATER

Of the swimming habits or abilities of bats, little has been scientifically documented. An abundance of anecdotal reports, some of them by naturalists, attest to a variety of bats having been seen swimming under a number of circumstances. Under appropriate circumstances, swimming may be part of the natural behavior of some bats. Many bats of course live close to water, fresh or salt. Many species dip low over ponds or streams when hunting insects. Others dip their mouths into the water to drink as they fly. Almost all cave-dwelling bats run the risk of falling into the pools or streams which are frequently found in their abodes.

While pursuing and capturing a large variety of bats in caves, I have seen them fall into the water on the floor, usually in panicked response to my presence, but I have never seen bats swimming under normal circumstances. I have always tried to rescue bats that have fallen into water, replacing them on dry roosts, or taking them along and caring for them. But in my experience, bats that have been soaked have never survived. Perhaps the sudden loss of body heat to the cool water may be an irreversible shock.

Fruit bats like the flying foxes and their smaller relatives rarely drink water; apparently they derive all the water they need from their moist food. Flying foxes, like the individual shown swimming vigorously on these pages, never live in caves but roost on the branches of tall trees. Thus one might expect them to have little or no need to swim.

On the other hand, flying foxes are largely island dwellers. They often fly considerable distances over water to feeding sites. Forced landings may occur and hence skill in swimming may be an advantage. In addition, water currents are responsible for the dispersal of a number of edible tropical fruit which drop into the water, float, and often collect along shores. Perhaps fruit bats occasionally land in the water while attempting to salvage this fruit.

With head held high—as much at home in the water as a dog—a flying fox, *Pteropus giganteus*, confidently makes its way through an element seemingly incongruous for an animal whose principal mode of locomotion is flight.

As these pictures show, the bat is not paddling amateurishly but definitely swimming. It may be benefitting from its wing membranes the way a snorkel swimmer uses artificial "flippers" to enhance the ability of his feet to move water. Heading towards land, the flying fox swims into the shallows and then begins to make its way out of the water.

This bat roosts in trees rather than caves, and therefore has to endure and survive inclement weather. Its coat is substantially waterproof; this fact, together with its relatively great size, may make it more likely to survive immersion than most bats.

HEAT ADDICTS

Heat lovers, *Tadarida molossa*, free-tailed bats of the American tropics, seek out crevices in buildings in which to roost. They prefer locations where they are shielded from the light of the sun but receive the full force of its radiant heat. Like many other free-tailed bats, *Tadarida* may seek out sun-baked roosts, especially in the late afternoon, to raise their body temperature in anticipation of, and preparation for, emerging at dusk. At the base of the thumb *Tadarida* have a pad to help bear the forearm weight. Moving freely forwards or backwards, the bat keeps its wings tightly folded. In slow movement, only one limb is raised at a time, but when speed is called for, one foot and the opposite wrist move simultaneously.

Unlike most free-tailed bats, *Tadarida molossa* roost communally but individually spaced out. When one animal finds its path blocked by the presence of another, as in the case of the confrontation shown here, a sham battle may take place. The bats will adopt belligerent postures and utter threatening cries but the "battles" usually end, as this one does, with one of the contenders retreating.

THE ACROBATICS CHAMPION

Vampires are the champion acrobats of the order. They have good reason to be. They often roost in places where flight is difficult or impossible. Agility on the ground and the ability to leap are assets in tight spots. Also, the species shown here, *Desmodus rotundus*, is small (an adult weighs about one ounce or thirty grams), yet preys on large livestock. Even a gentle kick by the intended victim or a swish of the tail could be fatal to a bat that could not swiftly dodge. Vampires advance on their targets as circumspectly as possible, on foot. They may assume a variety of walking postures. They may even walk almost upright, as shown here. Their extra-long forearms, which seem to be an adaptation for walking or jumping, bear weight on three pads: one on the wrist, one at the base of the thumb, and one at the end.

Overleaf: A number of vampires display their skill, unequaled among bats, at jumping.

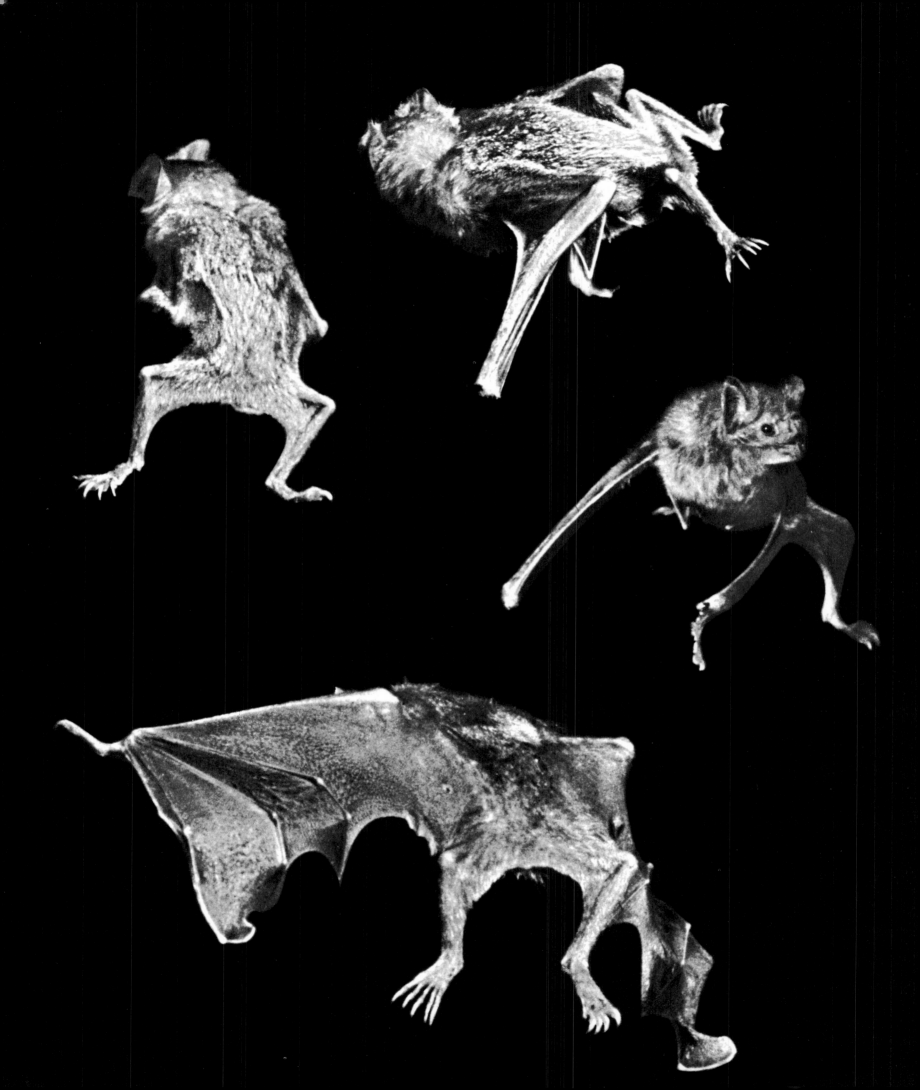

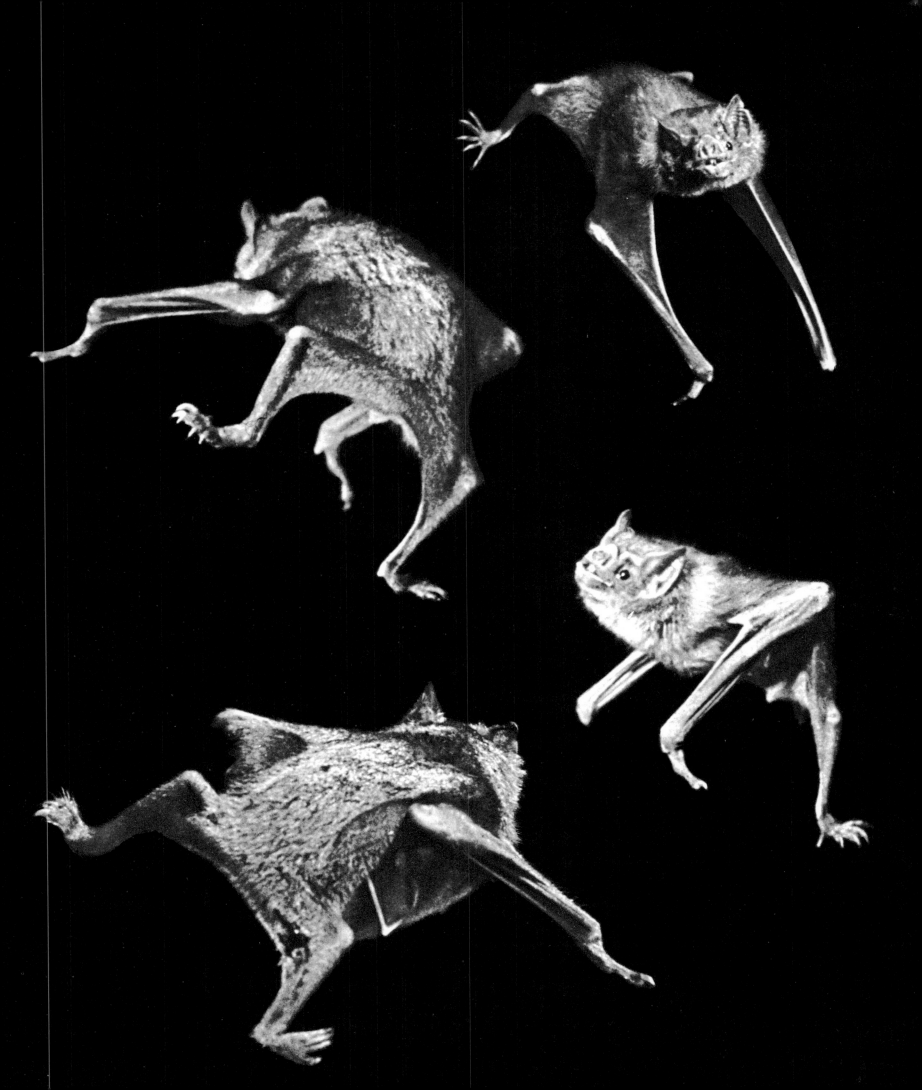

A BIG-EARED CRAWLER

Apart from the striking ears, the most conspicuous features of the spotted bat is its coloration. It has three white spots on its dark back, making for a polka-dot effect. Very few bats are so vividly marked. All other bats as distinctively marked as this one roost in the open, where they can be seen as they rest or sleep. The markings seem to serve as camouflage, breaking up the visible outline of the body. The spots of this bat may serve the same function as do the stripes of zebras or tigers, which seem to draw attention until they are seen in the animals' natural terrain of brightly contrasting sunlight and shadow. Spotted bats are still poorly understood, but from their markings we may assume that they too roost at times in full view.

Spotted bats, *Euderma maculata*, probably roost in crevices of boulder heaps, under rocks, in or on desert vegetation, or in the burrows of other animals. All of these choices of habitat call for crawling, a mode of locomotion at which the spotted bat is adept.

At left, the animal has found a place in a hollow rock in which to sleep, and its outsized, translucent ears are partly furled. Above, the bat emerges and the ears are unfurled, being brought to attention. Furling the ears not only serves to protect them from injury but may also help to camouflage the bat and conserve body heat.

Its ears now fully erect and huge in proportion to the size of the rest of it, the spotted bat continues to explore its rocky environment, crawling and observing with great deliberation and caution.

Euderma maculata examines a drop. Apparently deciding not to chance it, the bat moves back and *(below)* proceeds to crawl circumspectly in a less vertical direction.

Four bats here demonstrate versatility in getting around. At left, a flying fox moves backwards up a branch, using both feet and both thumbs. At bottom left, another flying fox hangs by its strong and mobile thumbs instead of the usual way of hanging by its feet; in this position the animal is of course upside down—for a bat. Opposite page: a hoary bat twirls around to adjust its hold on a twig as it prepares to roost.

Rousettus aegyptiacus, the dog-faced bat, climbs forward along a branch using all four limbs *(below)*. The first toe of the right foot is being used independently. (Many bats have independent control of their toes.)

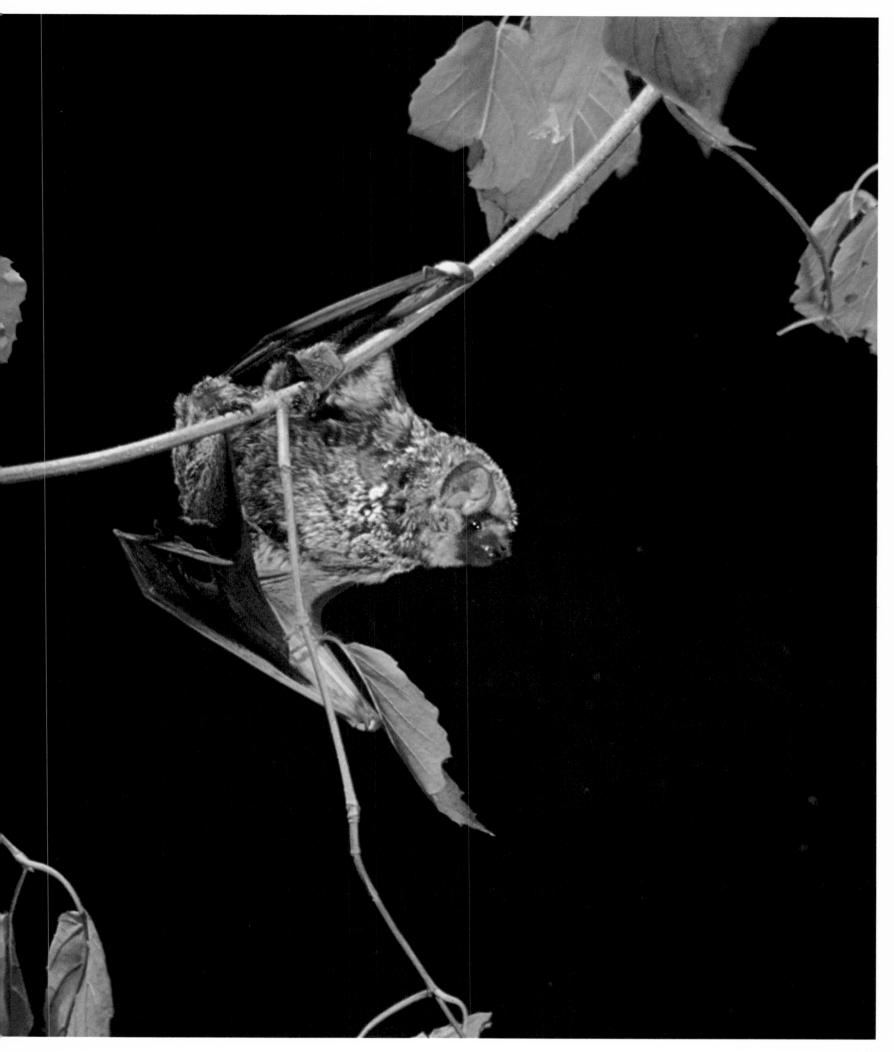

A Malaysian short-nosed fruit bat, *Cynopterus brachyotis*, roosts on a banana leaf, its wings wrapped around its belly and chest. Its feet are in opposite orientations. Bats of this suborder, the Megachiroptera, are the only ones which roost with their backs to the object on which they hang. To take flight, they let go with one foot and flip over, rotating on the other leg to bring their back and wings uppermost.

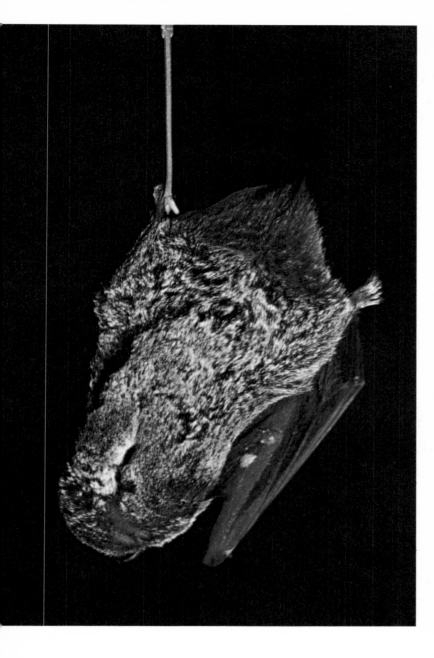

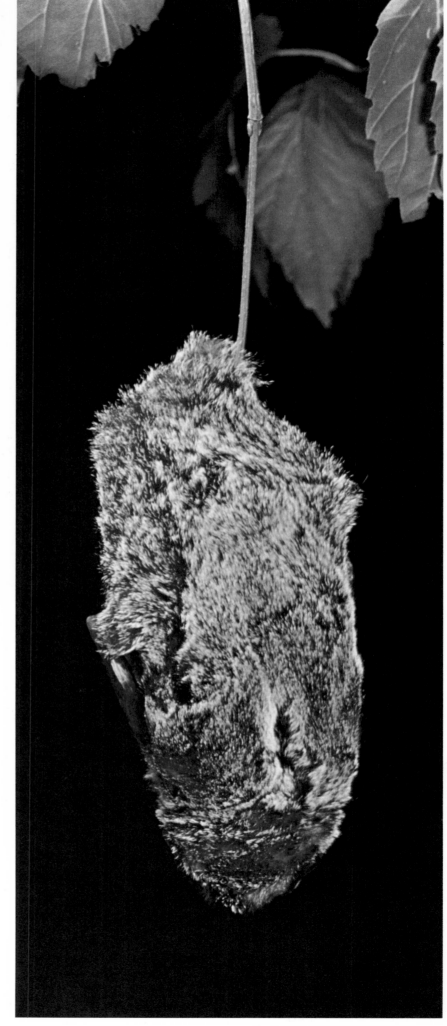

he hoary bat is difficult to detect when roosting and has seldom been
scovered in this posture even by experienced naturalists. While it is still
ttling down, one wing is visible *(above)*, but when the bat is in full repose
ight) it is enveloped in deep frost-tipped fur, which blends in with the li-
ens and mosses that grows on the bark of the trees that hoary bats inhabit.

Not all four of the bats seen on these pages are asleep but the pictures do show the positions they assume for sleeping. At left, an African giant leaf-nosed bat, *Hipposideros commersoni gigas*, hangs with a foot clutching each side of a branch. Its wings are folded alongside the body, its tail lies back to keep the interfemoral membrane out of the way. Below, a flying fox, asleep, has enveloped itself in its wings and tucked its head up against its chest, perhaps to shut out the light. Its color pattern seems to be of the sort known as countershading. Seen from above by a predator, the bat would be dark brown or black against the dark forest floor. Seen from below, it would be gold against the brilliantly lighted tropical sky.

At left, a Jamaican flower bat, *Phyllonycteris aphylla*, sleeps securely—though seemingly precariously—clinging lightly to a branch by the claws of its toes. The wings are held in a partly folded posture. In repose above is an African epaulette bat, *Epomophorus*, grasping a branch from both sides.

An obvious penalty for roosting in the open rather than in caves or buildings is inclement weather. Here a flying fox endures a rainstorm. At first the head is left exposed, but then (above) the wings are elevated, apparently to protect the head and face.

ECHOLOCATION

Acoustic orientation or echolocation is the only feature of bat life which has been investigated in a major fashion. As noted earlier, the genus *Rousettus* are the only Megachiroptera to orient acoustically. *Rousettus* use audible pulses of sound produced by tongue clicking and depend on echoes from these sounds for guidance in the dark. Producing no sounds in flight, other Megachiroptera apparently find their way by vision and olfaction. How they manage to forage when there is no light, or very little, is not known.

Bats of the genus *Rousettus* have evolved a sonar system independently of the Microchiroptera. All of the bats of the suborder Microchiroptera, insofar as they have been studied, echolocate and depend on echolocation for tracking insects or other prey and for avoiding obstacles. Those which feed on fruit, flowers or vertebrates (which emit odors) probably also use olfactory information for local orientation but their sonar system is nevertheless of prime importance. The Microchiroptera all send out intensely loud, ultrashort pulses of high frequency sound which are reflected by objects in their path. We have studied such sounds, from a wide variety of bats, in terms of their major parameters: frequency, frequency pattern, pulse duration, pulse-repetition rate, interpulse interval, intensity, and directionality. In all of the Microchiroptera studied so far, the pulses are produced in the larynx.

BEAMING THE SOUND

Depending upon the species, the sounds are emitted through the mouth or the nostrils. In bats which emit their sonar pulses nasally, the larynx often fits into the nasopharynx, mechanically separating the air passage from the mouth and from food and water being swallowed. Many, if not all, of the bats which regularly emit their orientation pulses nasally have a nose leaf. This may serve either to beam the sounds into a forward, compact, conelike shape or it may instead deflect sound from a retrograde path to the bat's own ears. In some bats the nose leaf may even serve to cast an echo shadow of some sort on the ears.

Many bats emit their sonar signals orally. Some of these, like the mustache bats, form their mouth and lips into a megaphone shape when doing so. Generally, they lack a nose leaf. The nasal emitters usually have rather short, flat faces, with the cranial-facial proportions of higher Primates or Pekingese dogs. Oral-emitting bats usually have distinct or even elongate snouts and are often likened to dogs or rodents.

Bats' sonar signals do not spread in all directions equally. Very little of the sound can be detected behind, above, or below the animal. The greatest sound pressures occur in something less than a hemisphere in front of the bat's mouth or nose. Sound travels in air at about 345 m/sec and is intercepted by objects in the foreground: insects, trees, leaves, houses, and the ground, to mention a few. Sound may be reflected from the surface of such objects but may also, in part, be transmitted or absorbed. The proportion of sound reflected is largely determined by the dimensions of the object relative to the wave lengths of sound involved, by the surface texture and by the nature of the material or materials. In general, objects large enough to be of interest to bats, perhaps 1 mm or more, adequately reflect the wavelengths being used. Some of the reflected sound reaches one or usually both of the bat's ears and is perceived and processed by the ears and by acoustic interpretation centers in the brain. The information received appears to be adequate to identify the direction, velocity, distance, and some elements of the "nature" of the reflecting surface. We do not yet understand how bats identify the characteristics of reflecting objects by analyzing the echoes. We do, however, have scatterings of solid evidence, lots of clues, and some interesting guesses.

DIRECTIONAL EARS

Bats' external ears are not only large but are usually highly mobile. From studies on several genera, we also know their ears to be highly directional. That is, sounds coming from certain directions are received optimally while sounds from other directions are partially blocked or attenuated. The optimal angle for the right ear (in the horizontal plane) might be 30° to the right of the midline while the least-favored angle for the same ear might be 120° to the left of the midline. Presumably bats assess the direction of a sound-reflecting object by comparing the perceived intensity in the two ears. In ambiguous cases, they can make a series of judgments with the ears and head in different positions. We know from the elegant electrophysiological experiments performed by Alan Grinnel, while a graduate student at Harvard, that this sort of mechanism is used by at least some bats. The sound processing centers of the brain are alerted by the reception of a sound either slightly earlier or at a slightly higher intensity by one ear than by the other and this asymmetry activates other analytical processes.

The middle ear of bats, as of other mammals, conveys sound from the eardrum to the actual sense organ of the inner ear. The eardrum or tympanic membrane vibrates in response to sound waves impinging on it and transmits these vibrations to a chain of three tiny bones, the auditory ossicles. The innermost of these bones, the stapes, has a footplate resting against a membranous window in the bony wall of the fluid-bathed inner ear. The sound waves are transmitted via the auditory ossicles to this oval window. The relative areas of the tympanic membrane and the window plus the leverlike action of the auditory ossicles provide mechanical advantage which links the airborne sound waves of the external ear canal efficiently into the fluid of the inner ear.

THE INNER EAR

Two small but active muscles reside in the middle ear. One, the tensor tympani, alters the posture of the outermost ossicle, the malleus, and the tension of the eardrum. The other, the stapedius, alters the posture of the stapes on the oval window. In all mammals, these muscles contract when extra loud sounds are heard or while the animal itself is barking or speaking, yawning or swallowing. Their function seems to be to protect the inner ear from disruptive stimulation. When the muscles are contracted, the chain of ossicles is stabilized and the transmission of sound is diminished.

In bats, we now know, from experiments carried out at Yale by O'Dell W. Henson, Jr., that the middle ear muscles

contract before each sonar pulse is emitted and apparently serve to attenuate the intensity of each outgoing pulse that reaches the bat's own ear. The muscles usually relax in time to optimize echo reception. Thus bats have adapted a previously available mechanism for reducing the perceived intensity of outgoing pulses but not of the returning echoes.

From the beginning of the modern studies of bat orientation we wondered how bats could hear faint echoes so quickly after emitting intense outgoing pulses of sound. We now have several answers to this question and more answers probably still await recognition. Not only do the middle ear muscles favor echo reception by their carefully coordinated contractions but the ears (the entire encapsulated complex of inner and middle ear bones) are often quite isolated from the skull. In most mammals, the otic capsules are fused solidly to the skull. In some bats, the otic capsules float in rather loose attachment to the skull, isolated and insulated by fatty connective tissue or by blood-filled sinuses. (The otic capsules often fall out of cleaned bat skulls that are kept in museum study collections and are easily lost.) This isolation from the skull presumably reduces bony conduction of sound from the bat's own larynx and respiratory passages to its ears. It also would improve the isolation of one ear from the other for the assessment of direction. I shall refer to other echo-favoring adaptations later.

THE "TICKLAUT"

The orientation pulses which bats emit are predominantly of ultrasonic frequencies. Some sheath-tailed bats produce frequencies audible to man (as low as 12 KHz) along with more intense higher harmonics. Other bats generally produce frequencies above 20 KHz. Men generally hear only up to about 18 or 20 KHz though young children may be sensitive to slightly higher frequencies. A former colleague of mine reports that in his childhood in India he was often kept awake by the loud and ubiquitous sounds of bats hawking by his bedroom windows. His nurse, much older of course and with more limited hearing, perennially refused to believe his excuse for remaining awake. But even adults, sitting quietly in a well isolated room and listening attentively while bats fly by, can ear a faint but clear component of the sonar signals called the *ticklaut*. In some bats, cold molossids for example, the *ticklaut* is particularly prominent. Were we sensitive to the principal compononts of bat pulses, we would be substantially discommoded, for these are produced at astonishingly high intensities.

CF AND FM

Many bats produce orientation pulses which we describe as frequency modulated. Such pulses sweep downward in frequency, often by about one octave. Thus they may start at 80 KHz and sweep rather regularly down to 40 KHz at their termination. Vespertilionids, molossids, and natalids, among others, produce pulses of this sort. The exact frequency range varies with species and, among the vespertilionids, also sometimes seems to vary among individuals and from pulse to pulse. In the molossids, the highest fundamental frequency is usually relatively modest, often 60 KHz or less. Among the vespertilionids, sweeps starting as high as 120 KHz have been recorded. The common range, however, would be 60 to 80 KHz sweeping to 30 to 40 KHz. The fundamental sweep is often accompanied by a second and even a third harmonic sweep, one and two octaves higher. FM bats have at their disposal quite a variety of frequencies and wavelengths.

Other bats produce pulses consisting of a constant frequency (CF) portion followed by a brief frequency modulated (FM) termination. In *Chilonycteris parnellii*, for example, the CF portion, at about 32 KHz, may last for 18 msec and is followed by a 2 msec FM portion. In *Rhinolophus*, long CF portions, often 30 to 40 msec, are followed by brief frequency sweeps. In most of these bats, the CF portion is characterized by at least two prominent components, the fundamental and its second harmonic, an octave higher. Thus in *C. parnellii* the second harmonic of 64 KHz is present. There are variations in these patterns. In the slit-faced bats and the Old World false vampires, for example, the short orientation pulses are of constant frequency but with several prominent harmonics. Many of the sheath-tailed bats use slightly frequency modulated sweeps with prominent harmonics.

What determines the frequency range used by a particular species of bat or by bats in general? Perhaps an important consideration in selecting ultrasonic frequencies is the low level of the ambient ultrasonic noise. It seems likely that relatively few interfering sounds, insect songs principally, would be widespread or conspicuous in this frequency band. Perhaps the use of the ultrasonic frequency range avoids attracting predators. On the other hand, higher frequency sound is attenuated by air. By 100 KHz such attenuation is substantial. So perhaps these considerations counterbalance each other.

The frequency of pulses may simply be dictated by the dimensions of the sound-generating organs. The smaller and the tenser the membranes, the higher the frequencies produced. One might guess that small bats (hence small larynges) would produce higher frequencies, but this is often not the case.

In general, one might expect small bats to feed on small prey and large bats on large prey. We do not know this to be true though there ought to be some such tendency and, if it does exist, then small bat species ought to favor high frequencies, other things being equal. The higher the frequency, the shorter the wavelength. Objects with dimensions of about one wavelength seem to reflect sound especially effectively. A wavelength at 100 KHz in air is about 3.5 mm. At 30 KHz, the wavelength is about 11.5 mm. Few naturally interesting objects would be less than 3.5 mm in diameter. Spider web strands, an interesting example, are poorly detected by bat sonar systems and several ultrasmall species of bats are reported to become entangled in them. Again, few edible objects for the majority of bats are much larger than one or two cm in diameter. Fruit, flowers, and vertebrates are probably detected by a different system, i.e., by olfaction. Therefore the range of wavelengths seems roughly appropriate. Of course, large obstacles also have to be detected.

HITS AND MISSES

Actually, in their ability to detect objects, bats are not limited to those larger than 3.5 mm in diameter. Bats of several families have now been observed in detail while traversing an obstacle course. Such a course usually consists of a plane of vertically hung wires spaced somewhat less than a wing-spread apart. A bat is forced to fly repeatedly through the obstacle plane and its score is recorded in terms of hits and misses. Agile individuals of most species avoid wires with diameters down to 0.1 or even 0.08 mm with better than chance scores. Since such wires are often of the order of 1/30th of a wavelength, these are impressive performances.

The orientation pulses of all bats are short in duration but a considerable variation occurs. The horseshoe bats may produce 50 or 60 msec pulses. Hipposiderids and some mustache bats also use long pulses, often over 20 msec. The Nycteridae and the Megadermatidae, on the other hand, use pulses of 1 msec or less. In fact, I have recorded pulses from them which were less than 0.5 msec in duration.

MEASURING DURATION

We now know that, for meaningful analysis, pulse durations must be measured while the bat is engaged in a biologically significant sequence. That is, pulse durations vary significantly during series of events such as insect pursuits, approaches to and avoidance of obstacles, and landings where the anticipated perch is chosen from some distance.

Students of bat behavior have succeeded in studying insect pursuits or other sequential events in only a few genera. In these, however, we now have some understanding of the functions of pulse duration. In *Chilonycteris psilotis*, for example, the pulses produced during what we call cruising or searching flight are about 4 msec in duration. These bats, when hunting fruitflies in the laboratory, show the first signs of beginning pursuit—by shortening orientation pulses and increasing the repetition rate—when they are about 600 mm from the insect. Sound travels at about 345 mm/msec. A 4 msec pulse, therefore, has a length in air of about 1380 mm. Since sound has to make a round trip for the echoes to be perceived, echoes from any object closer than 690 mm will overlap at the bat's ear with the outgoing pulse. That is, the echo will return from an object within 690 mm before the pulse has been fully emitted. Thus, *C. psilotis* detect an insect or at least have their attention directed to a given insect when its echo overlaps with the outgoing pulse.

Given a species-characteristic searching-pulse duration of 4 msec, objects will always be detected when they are about 600 mm away. Such a system means that distance (at least for prey pursuits) need never be quantified or measured. Everything beyond 600 mm can be categorized as "distant." Perhaps distant objects need not even be perceived. Perhaps they are perceived and not responded to by the criteria we have used to assess response. Everything that produces an echo which overlaps with the outgoing pulse would be in a narrow band, perhaps 100 mm wide, which we might label as "approaching." No unnoticed objects can be closer than this overlap band since they would then have been detected by previous pulses and would therefore have previously fixed the bat's attention. Pulse intensity may be adapted for detecting objects of interesting size at this species-specific hunting range. That is, the intensity may be adjusted so as to ensure echoes of adequate amplitude for objects of edible size at 600 mm.

Pulse repetition rate and flight speed must also be considered in connection with fixed, search-phase pulse duration such as are seen in *C. psilotis*. If the bat produces about 18 pulses per second, then a silent interval of about 55 msec during which the bat moves forward about 100 mm, follows each pulse. Let us assume that the bat had just missed detecting an insect with its previous pulse. Now it emits a second pulse. An object previously just beyond overlap range (that is, 700 mm away), will now be about 600 mm from the bat. The echo will now overlap by 0.6 msec with the outgoing pulse. If the insect is flying directly away from or toward the bat, if the bat's flight speed is irregular, if the pulse durations vary, or if interpulse intervals vary substantially, the amount of overlap and the depth of the detection band will vary but not by very much. Pulse-repetition rate or interpulse interval appear to be set in the search phase for sampling of the foreground.

INTERCEPTION

Having detected an insect, *C. psilotis* alters its flight path to intercept it, and, at the same time, increases the pulse petition rate (decreases interpulse interval) and cuts pulse durations. The pursuit and capture of an insect at this range takes perhaps 250 to 350 msec. About 200 msec are consumed by what we call the approach phase, during which the pulse-repetition rate rises to about 100 per second. The last 75 msec or so are devoted to what we call the terminal phase, in which the pulse repetition rate rises to 170 per second or more. The terminal phase is also called the "buzz," which describes our subjective perception when we hear the audible *ticklaut* during pursuit or listen to a pursuit via a transducer. In *C. psilotis*, the pulse duration drops off linearly with target distance. We have calculated, from the bat's position relative to the target insect as each pulse is emitted, what the overlap is and we have found that pulse duration is so set each time as to give about msec of overlap between the outgoing pulse and the returning echo. Thus the bat is regularly assessing distance and presumably derives some advantage from regulation of pulse duration by target distance. No absolute measure of distance is really required, only an indication initially that there is a target at the usual range and then that the bat is closing on the target as anticipated. So one function of pulse duration may be supposed to be the evaluation of distance.

In the closely related *C. parnellii*, search-phase pulses are about 20 msec in duration. These bats also seem to have their attention drawn to insect targets by pulse-echo overlap but because their pulses are longer, the overlap occurs initially at about 3.5 m. Pulse duration, therefore, also determines hunting range. Calculations based on observed repetition rates and flight speed lead to much the same conclusions as with *C. psilotis*. During the search phase, pulses are emitted just often enough to screen or probe the foreground sequentially as the bat moves forward.

Following detection of an insect at 3.5 m, *C. parnellii* first increase their pulses to about 32 msec and then start to decrease them linearly with closing target distance. The initial overlap is about 1 to 2 msec, but after the pulses have been lengthened, overlaps of about 20 msec occur. Long overlaps, declining to about 5 msec late in the terminal phase, characterize the insect pursuits of this species. What do such long overlaps signify? Recent experiments by Dr. Henson indicate that the long, CF portion of the *C. parnellii* pulse has an important effect on

the sound-processing centers of the brain. Henson's studies involved implanting electrodes in the brains of bats, especially in the posterior colliculus, a tertiary sound-processing center, and using these electrodes to record brain activity. The bats are prepared under anesthesia, of course, but are observed while fully awake and behaving normally. The experimental techniques are fascinating and ingenious but too technically detailed to describe here.

INTERPULSE INTERVAL

In one interesting experimental sequence, the bat flew across a room to an isolated landing perch and directed its sonar attention to locating this perch. The sequence of pulses in such a landing is similar to that in an insect pursuit. Brain activity was low during the emission and perception of the CF portions of the pulses. Evoked potentials, probably representing echo responses, were observed only during the interpulse interval. About three large evoked responses were observed between pulses early in the landing sequence. Later, only two evoked responses seemed to fit into the interpulse interval and, finally, only one evoked response appeared. The outgoing pulse (at least the CF portion), seemed to block brain activity. The brain appeared to be "turned down" during the high amplitude output, thus avoiding "wasting" its sensitivity in responding to the outgoing sound. In addition, the brain was turned down again after perceiving the third (or later the first) echo. Information reaching the brain during the interpulse interval was therefore processed in a different way from information feeding in during pulse emission. Initially, at a distance, the bat may have been plotting the positions of several objects —the perch, the wall, and so forth. As the bat closed on the perch, it seemed to close down the interpulse interval to "focus" on the first of the returning echoes. That is, it was excluding echoes or reverberations from more distant objects. A shallow depth of field would naturally leave the bat vulnerable were it to be continued for long but we are speaking of a period of less than a second. Presumably the bat can open up the interval if there is some reason to do so—such as the intrusion of unexpected sounds or echoes. Thus, in *C. parnellii* the increased pulse duration and decreased interpulse interval appear to have a function in refining depth of field.

But what significance does the long overlap have?

Some of the evoked responses come not at the beginning of overlap (indeed few, if any, do) but during the interpulse interval. From Henson's work and that of Grinnell as well, we know that acoustic processing neurons respond in a variety of ways to the CF pulses: some respond to the "on," some to the "off," and some to the continuation of CF pulses if the continuation is long enough, perhaps over 6 msec. The system in *C. parnellii* may be designed to use long CF pulses to influence functionally the responsiveness of differently designed neurons. I believe that the purpose of lengthening the pulses on detection is to separate out two echo functions. First, the CF echo is received and processed (perhaps to assess velocity by Doppler shift); then the FM echo is received (perhaps to assess target direction). The way the bat regulates pulse duration during the approach phase holds these two functions separate and temporarily fixed relative to one another.

ALTERATION BY DOPPLER SHIFT

In *C. parnellii*, during the approach phase, the echo CF would be altered by Doppler shift which is imposed by the relative velocities of the bat and its target. The difference in frequencies, if it were being measured, would give a measure of relative velocity. The difference in frequencies might also remove the echo frequency from competition with the output frequency.

From the electrophysiology experiments of Nobuo Suga and Grinnell, we know that many neurons of the posterior colliculus have sharply tuned frequency sensitivity. From Henson's and from Grinnell's experiments we also know that the audiogram in *C. parnellii* (a curve representing threshold of hearing) rises sharply immediately adjacent to the principal output frequencies (about 32 and 64 KHz respectively). That is, the bat's perception system is sharply tuned. Suppose it is so sharply tuned that many of the neurons do not respond to the output frequency (say 32 kc) but to the Doppler-shifted

echo frequency instead (perhaps 32.4 KHz). This would be another echo-favoring refinement. H. U. Schnitzler, a student of Möhres in Tubingen, has shown that horseshoe bats can respond to Doppler shift by altering their output. That is to say, when a horseshoe bat, which normally produces pulses of 80 KHz, detects an approaching insect (the echo from which will be slightly higher than 80 KHz), it reduces its output frequency just enough to bring the echo back to 80 KHz. In this way it may hold the echoes in its prime sensitivity band while at the same time moving the output frequency into a region of insensitivity.

Not all bats operate with pulse durations designed to produce pulse-echo overlaps. In addition to the mustache bats, *Rhinolophus* and *Hipposideros* apparently do so. The vespertilionids, on the other hand, alter their pulse duration (also by shortening it) during insect pursuits or obstacle course traversals so as to preclude pulse-echo overlap. *Noctilio*, the fishing bulldog bat, also shortens its pulses during sequences of echolocation of fish in the laboratory but again sufficiently to preclude pulse-echo overlap. We do not at present know enough to interpret these different designs.

Pulse-repetition rates are of the order of 10 to 20 per second during searching flight and up to 200 per second or more during the terminal phase of insect pursuits. I have already presented the concrete evidence we have which bears on the function of repetition rate. Now I should like to speculate further and suggest: 1. that searching-repetition rates represent economy of output; 2. that approach-phase repetition rates allow an increased flow of some needed kind of information (perhaps the direction of the insect or landing perch and/or its velocity as well as details of the presence of other nearby objects); and 3. that terminal-repetition rates exclude most information except that coming from the target and maximize information on target location and closing target distance.

PAINFUL NOISE LEVELS

Orientation pulses are, in an absolute sense, always very loud. The human threshold of hearing at our best frequencies is expressed as being at about 0.0002 dynes/cms. The threshold hearing in bats is about the same at their best frequencies, which are usually close to the most prominent frequencies of their output. The faintest bat orientation pulses known are about 1 dyne/cm² when recorded at about 5 cm from the bat's mouth or nose. Rather loud bats produce pulses at 100 or 00 dynes/cms. These are truly intense sounds, comparable with offensive or even painful noise levels in civilization such as those of subways, jet engines, or boiler factories.

Sound spreads in three dimensions from its source. This means that there is an ever increasing front of sound and a resulting dissipation or attenuation of the sound at any interrupting point. Only a small portion of a bat's sound output is reflected by an insect; the reflected sound also spreads in three dimensions and continues to be attenuated as well. Thus the returning echo is faint relative to the outgoing pulse. But the returning echo from objects at appropriate distances is loud enough to be perceived and analyzed by the bat. The output must be sufficiently intense to serve adequately for the ranges and object sizes that the bat works with. Bats which fly in the open, especially at high altitudes, and hunt flying insects use high amplitude outputs. High amplitude, in general, also goes with long pulse duration, probably associated with long hunting ranges.

WHISPERING BATS

Bats which fly in the jungle or in the jungle canopy and those which fly close to walls, tree trunks, or the ground seeking roosting victims use relatively low amplitude pulses. We often call these the whispering bats. Some hunt at short range and thus avoid attenuation loss. In addition, they conserve energy, reduce the output effect on their sound processing centers, and perhaps utilize an optimal echo-intensity band. Other whispering bats do not hunt at very short range but appear to be faced instead by an excessively complex environment—vines, branches, leaves, and thorns. I reason that in such circumstances they may gain advantage by reducing output intensity so as to set a limit on the range from which echo information will return. Perhaps these bats can process echoes from three objects at a time or from ten or even more but there must be

a practical limit. By reducing the output intensity, they concentrate their attention on the closest objects and exclude the rest. Such a system, of course, requires slow, deliberate flight so as to preclude collisions with obstacles which have not yet been examined and to assure "seeing" an adequate proportion of food objects before they have been passed by. In fact, whispering bats can normally hover or fly slowly. (High-amplitude bats generally fly swiftly and are relatively unable to maneuver.) Whispering bats also usually use short-duration pulses. Their hunting range is relatively short and, whether they use or preclude overlap, short pulses serve them best.

It may seem strange that I refer to whispering bats after having said that all bats use pulses of high intensity. Those which use relatively low intensities, especially if they use high frequencies, are technically hard to study. Our microphones, even today, are relatively insensitive in the frequency band of bat-orientation pulses and are often progressively less sensitive as the frequency increases. Thus, bats are "whisperers" when we find it hard to record their output.

The initial studies of the bat sonar system by Griffin dealt entirely with North American vespertilionids, particularly *Myotis* and *Eptesicus*. In 1953, he went to Panama to survey the sonar systems of bats of several additional families. His experience with many of the spear-nosed bats (Phyllostomatidae) was frustrating. He was unable to record *any* sound output from several genera. His frustration paralleled that of Spallanzani 150 years before. How could a bat be echolocating unless it was producing orientation pulses and if it was producing such pulses why could they not be recorded? We now know that they *were* producing orientation pulses but Griffin's microphones were technically inadequate to record them.

During the next year, I joined Griffin's laboratory as a research fellow newly out of a residency in medicine. I began a series of experiments designed to identify the mechanisms of pulse production. Principally I systematically denervated the muscles of the larynx, the tongue, and the palate in order to localize the sound-producing motor organ or organs. The cricothyroid muscles of the larynx proved to be crucial in the vespertilionids, *Myotis* and *Eptesicus*. These bats, with the cricothyroid muscles denervated, emitted audible peeps only and were disoriented in flight.

AUDIBLE
AND DISORIENTED

At that time, we had some examples of the tropical, spear-nosed bat *Carollia* living in the laboratory. We had never heard them emit any orientation pulses. I operated on four of them and we were astonished to observe that *Carollia*, after cricothyroid denervation, were disoriented in flight and, for the first time, emitted audible peeps. Presumably the effect had been the same as in the vespertilionids—ultrasonic pulses had been replaced by useless sonic ones. Some of these *Carollia* survived and, several weeks after surgery, we were again astonished to find that one of them was no longer producing audible peeps. On listening with a microphone sensitive to higher frequencies, however, we found that the bat was now producing ultrasonic pulses and again oriented in flight. By expecting to find pulses and by searching for them in a known frequency band, we had favored the signal to noise ratio enough to detect the faint (as recorded) output.

I went to Panama briefly that summer and confirmed these observations on *Carollia* and several other phyllostomatid genera. They were all producing technically elusive ultra-sonic orientation pulses. Dr. Griffin and I published a paper in 1955 describing these pulses as best we could but our descriptions and analyses became obsolete by 1956.

In those days any significant advance in acoustic equipment often rendered recent experimental findings completely out of date. In the fall of 1955, for example, I undertook a trip to collect and study the bats of the Old World tropics. In the course of ten months I worked in the Philippines, Ceylon, and the Belgian Congo. I undertook the trip even though we were technically no better off than I had been in Panama the year before. About five months out, when I was in Ceylon, I heard from Dr. Griffin that he had had a new microphone built from plans which had recently appeared in an acoustical journal. He airmailed the microphone to me, along with its necessary power supply and other accessories. The new microphone, I discovered on the first day, made almost everything I had previously accomplished obsolete. My Philippine observations were irretrievable but I decided to restudy all the bats that I had previously covered in Ceylon.

The new microphone made possible the recording of highe[r] frequency and lower-intensity signals than previously and als[o] made it possible to record the output of many whispering ba[ts] when they were in flight. Previously I had had to handhol[d] them directly in front of the microphone, risking the productio[n] of all sorts of artifacts. In spite of even better microphon[es] today, many questions still remain unanswered.

AMPLIFYING
A PSEUDO-ECHO

In several places, I have referred to mechanisms for max[i]mizing the perception of echoes and minimizing the perceptio[n] of outgoing orientation pulses. Several additional mechanism[s] are known or postulated. Grinnell was able to show, an[d] Henson to confirm, that evoked potentials recorded from th[e] posterior colliculus favor the second of two closely paire[d] sounds. If, for example, one presents to a bat's ear a pair [of] sounds (simulating an outgoing pulse and returning echo[)] matched for all parameters, the response to the second of th[e] pair will be greatly enhanced. That is, by the time that th[e] responses to sound reach the posterior colliculus, brain proces[s]ing has amplified the pseudo-echo.

Suga has described the mechanics of another interestin[g] system in vespertilionids. He studied the response characte[r]istics of single cells in the posterior colliculus when variou[s] sounds were presented to the bat's ear. Many posterior co[l]licular neurons have sharply-tuned frequency sensitivity. A[t] threshold, they respond only to sounds of an exact frequenc[y] say 50 KHz. As the amplitude of the stimulating sound [is] increased, the cell responds to an increasingly broader band [of] frequencies; at high-stimulus amplitudes the cell may again b[e] non-responsive. Suga reasoned that this upper cut-off wa[s] caused by inhibitory effects of neighboring neurons whose ow[n] best frequencies were perhaps 48 and 52 KHz respectivel[y] When stimulated with 50 KHz at high amplitude, he reasone[d] these cells would respond and, being interconnected with ou[r] original neuron, would inhibit it. He pointed out that such [a] set of relationships would be very useful. When the bat wa[s] emitting a frequency-modulated pulse at high amplitude, each frequency perceived could inhibit the neurons next lower in frequency response and thus leave them unrefractory to perceive the incoming echoes several milliseconds later. The echo would also be FM but with the low intensity this sweep would not be sufficient to activate the inhibitory interactions.

TURNING CELLS
DOWN OR UP

We know of two more mechanisms which would favor echo reception. In bats as well as other mammals, a nerve tract runs from the acoustic processing centers called the olivary complex to the sensory cells of the inner ear. This tract in some way modifies the response characteristics of the sensory cells. We may guess that the sensory cells could be forewarned of an outgoing pulse and turned down, or that they could be turned up at the anticipated time of an echo.

Finally, many of the neurons of the acoustic nerve, leading to the brain from the inner ear sensory cells, fire spontaneously. Their spontaneous discharge rate can be slowed or speeded up in response to stimulation by sound. That is, two directions of influence are possible. But in addition, each neuron which has just discharged spontaneously remains refractory and cannot be stimulated for a short period thereafter (about 0.5 to 2 msec). This means that some neurons will have been spared "hearing" some outgoing pulses (at least in bats using ultrabrief pulses) because they were then refractory from having just previously fired spontaneously. These neurons will be fresh and responsive to returning echoes shortly thereafter even as other neurons, in their turn, become refractory. That is, a neuron which has just fired spontaneously would not be responsive to an outgoing pulse but would have regained its responsiveness by the time the echo returned. Thus a population of neurons in a responsive state for the reception of echoes is guaranteed.

SONAR IN BIRDS

Not surprisingly, echolocation has evolved in two genera of birds which nest in dark caves, *Collocalia*, the edible nest swiftlets of Southeast Asia, and *Steatornis*, the oil birds of tropical America. Both use rapidly repeated audible clicks for orientation in caves. Neither, so far as we know, uses echolocation outside or for the pursuit of prey. The oil birds feed nocturnally on palm and laurel fruit. The swiftlets catch flying insects during the day. Both groups show a number of interesting parallels with bat biology.

Among the swiftlets, several species echolocate and several do not. All are grouped in a single genus. The visual species often nest in cliff faces; they construct their nests of vegetation pasted together with the secretions of a special oral gland. Three species studied by Lord Medway are known to echolocate and all of these nest in dark caves. Swiftlets normally carry nesting material with their beak but these species must also emit their orientation clicks by mouth. Some rearrangement has occurred in each of the three known cases. One carries its nesting materials with its feet. One has given up using vegetation and, instead, plucks out its own feathers for use as nesting material. The third species, the commercially important, edible-nest swiftlet, uses glandular secretions alone for building its nest. Thus all three have independently solved the apparent conflict between the two demands on their mouth.

We reason that echolocation must have evolved quite recently in *Collocalia* and we are now studying their brains and their acoustic physiology in an attempt to depict the early stages of development of such an elegant system.

APPENDIX

NOTES ON PHOTOGRAPHY ET CETERA

How do you follow bats to photograph their life in nature? Nobody can follow them at night on those long flights they take looking for food. Studies of bat behavior in nature are very limited. At night bat-watching is impossible, light beams would disturb them and make them move to another location and who could fly with them carrying cameras and lights? Even bats hunting their prey on the ground are impossible to observe at night.

It was clear to me that I had to meet them under controlled conditions to be able to observe their behavior and see how they would react to lights, cameras and myself, to know how fast or slow their movements were, to choose the right photo equipment, and to solve numerous problems I anticipated.

It was fortunate that the New York Zoological Garden had imported a group of flying foxes. With a camera and one small portable strobe-light (just in case) I came to the zoo to meet them. On this first day it appeared that the future would be very gloomy. In dark red light (it turns day into night for nocturnal animals), I could distinguish several shadows huddled together. To try focusing the lens was hopeless—in this light I could hardly see them without the camera. A dim white light had an even more frustrating result—they retreated as far back as they could.

Going back to the red light, I decided to wait. After a long while, my eyes got used to the red darkness. Now I could see them move their ears at the slightest sound, watching me steadily. As hours passed the situation did not change. They obviously hoped that I would not stay there forever. I assumed that offering them a plate filled with fruits would make a short trip from the branch worthwhile—but even this idea was not a success. By late afternoon I decided to give in and leave. I really did not know if our meetings would always be so uneventful, but I was not about to give up.

The next day they saw me back again. This time I intended to take some pictures before I left, even if it were only a test shot for lighting and exposure. With the glass between us, I estimated the distance to the spot they were watching me from, and with a small strobe-light synchronized to my Nikon I took a picture. The thought of a panic caused by a bright burst of light had frightened me. I did not want to upset them with my experiments. It seems I didn't. Nothing changed behind the glass front, the bats didn't move an inch. In some respects it encouraged me: it meant that strobe-light did not bother them, that I could use more lights and place them in the right positions. The next problem was to focus and

163

quickly refocus under red lighting. The difference in wave-length makes it quite difficult. To have a white light go on and off each time I had to refocus following their actions would undoubtedly ruin any hope of improving the already not-too-warm relations with my objects.

The solution I found in a small flashlight. Expecting them to move along the tree branches in their enclosure (if they would ever leave their observation post!), I directed a small beam on one of the branches and focused. If they moved only slightly forward or backward, I could refocus while shooting without using the flashlight again. It wasn't a foolproof solution, but it was a solution and it worked more often than I expected. Even later, when I found other ways of focusing, I never gave up using my flashlight.

Needless to say, this was another uneventful day. The bats watched my doings, they didn't object by hiding, didn't approve by moving around, didn't do a thing—they were just hanging and looking. By now they knew more about my behavior than I did about theirs.

Having solved some of my first technical problems all I could do the following day was to wait. This time they didn't think I deserved much attention. They knew what I would be doing—nothing unusual to concern them.

Being afraid to spoil the new harmony I avoided any actions which would put the bats again on guard. After all, they had just come to a foreign location and I was a part of it. Now it was time for them to start living in the most natural way they could under the present conditions and it was up to me to photograph their daily routines.

The first day they all looked alike to me but now I knew exactly who was who. I started to get involved in their private lives. I was very upset when a pregnant female lost her baby! A young male was my favorite; for some reason he did not get along with the rest of the group. One day I turned away to talk to the keeper when we heard a loud commotion. In the dark I could not see what had happened, but I instinctively turned my camera toward the trouble spot and started shooting. Looking at my developed film later I saw that the older bats turned on my young favorite—he was hurt, scared and retreated to a far corner. He died eventually and I felt that I lost somebody I was very fond of.

It was fortunate that the incident happened at the right distance from me and that I had the right lens on the camera. I always took with me several Nikons, each with a different focal length lens. Also, I feel much safer using more than one camera as insurance against any jinxes that could happen.

The results encouraged me to continue, but I also foresaw big problems: bats are not easy to keep in captivity because not enough experience has been accumulated about their diet. Very few American zoos had bats and if they did they were vampires and flying foxes. Blood for the vampires was easily available, and fruit-eaters like flying foxes could be fed in captivity for many years.

But what about all those other bats on my list, many of them insect eaters? Would they live long enough for me to take their pictures? I found out that naturalists kept them alive with a diet of mealworms, but even that was experimental—many bats died anyway. I assume that the shock of capture and confinement was too much to overcome. Most universities which use bats for their scientific studies needed only their bodies and had no need for facilities to keep and feed them.

To take pictures of nectar-feeders, I went to the University of Arizona, where Dr. E. Lendell Cockrum, Director of the Desert Biology Station of the University of Arizona, had made extensive studies of *Leptonycteris*. He arranged to make it possible for me to photograph these bats. A day before my arrival his students collected about twenty *Leptonycteris* from thirty miles away. On the university grounds, connected to a small room, was a large screened outdoor enclosure where the bats could fly around. During the day I set up my lights around a saguaro cactus whose flowers open at night and have a nectar favored by *Leptonycteris*.

I had my Nikon, with a 250-exposure motorized back, and I intended to use three repetitive strobe-lights, with one of them stronger for special lighting effects. The existing power unit had only two lights of equal strength. I had discussed my problem with Al Schneider, *Life's* equipment expert, and he had promised to think about it. He did. Next day he suggested adding another repetitive power supply of equal strength but to use only one light on this one. The synchronized circuits were interconnected so that they all fired together.

It was just getting dark when I finished all my prepparations. A dim light coming from the adjoining room replaced the red "night-light." The bats were hanging high up on the screen, sleeping or resting. These bats usually start feeding long after dark, sometimes close to midnight, the time when the saguaro blooms.

From reading and from my own observations I knew that after awakening bats start extensive cleaning of their wings and bodies. This sometimes lasts from fifteen to thirty minutes. Unreasonably hopeful, I was listening for early sounds of stirring—maybe the change in their environment might make a difference in their living pattern. From about 10 o'clock on I was constantly checking up on conditions by stepping from the little room into the outdoor enclosure, but nothing was moving. The bats and the cactus were equally dormant.

Shortly before 11 o'clock the bats began to move. In a quick beam of my flashlight I could see them cleaning and stretching themselves. The bats were exactly on time but for the cactus it was too early. The flowers were still closed. Perhaps the now unnecessary trip to the feeding grounds explained the wrong coordination? This was my theory and I started to worry about what would happen when the hungry bats swooped down and found the flowers tightly closed. I did not know if a similar situation happened to them in nature and whether they would know what to do. Later, when the first bats flew over to the cactus, they expertly opened the buds and got to the nectar. By the time the rest of the bats finished their grooming and came down to feed, the flowers were fully in bloom. I was shooting about three frames a second in sequences, the camera-motor noise did not disturb them and they might as well have been feeding in the desert! After the banquet all bats returned to the roosts.

Encouraged by their healthy appetites, I decided to offer them other flowers the next night: agaves and a century plant. I knew that they feed on the nectar of agave but the century plant was an experiment. The deep orange color of the plant was worthy a try! This night instead of the saguaro they would find those plants to choose from.

This evening I did not check up on them. Expecting them to awaken at the usual time I was busy potting the century plant. Suddenly I was surrounded, bats were all around me, some were landing on the large pockets of my jumper, reaching inside and hurriedly flying off.

The century plant was a big success; they landed, five or six at a time, to drink from the small orange blossoms. Agave was next on the menu. One thing was sure—the little nectar-feeders did not lose their appetite or show any other signs of discomfort. When I finished my shooting, they were released to fly home. I hope they made it.

Reading about vampires had made me particularly interested to see the variety of their movements. Reports like "... they can hop and jump like frogs—the only bats able to do it..." sounded fascinating. I couldn't find pictures of those jumps and it was a challenge to try.

The vampires in the zoos of Houston and Cincinnati live in roomy, manmade caves. Their faces are not exactly photogenic but they have alert and rational expressions. What impressed me most was their resemblance, in build, walk and fur color, to monkeys and apes.

The vampires can leap in all directions and where and when it happens only they can decide. Their jumps are unpredictable and so fast that I realized that they had jumped only after it had happened. This project of mine took a lot of time and patience. I had to work in both

A perfect jump! Only the vampires can jump like frogs.

zoos to get the pictures. Some days nobody jumped. On a "lucky" day I got parts of jumping vampires: they jumped right out of the frame. At the start I used a 36-exposure, motorized Nikon. Later I used a motorized Nikon with 250 exposures to be ready for the unexpected—the film was running but the bats were not jumping.

After frustrating hours my patience paid off. I did get several frames of postures that are never seen because they happen too fast.

One of the pictures in my script was a flying fox swimming. I had read in an Australian publication about them "easily swimming to shore." Considering it quite unusual locomotion for a bat, I assumed that all other flying foxes could probably swim as well. Mr. John Werler, Director of the Houston zoo, was willing to let me use a pond in a new, still unfinished aviary. It was a charming place with trees, ponds and a variety of plants under a giant glass roof. Houston had a large collection of flying foxes and one of them was selected for this experiment. I realized that the bat could take off any time before or after the swim—but it was a warm, lovely place for a bat to fly around and enjoy a short period of freedom and I really hoped she would. She did—but luckily not before I had taken my pictures.

Using a motorized camera, I balanced daylight with synchronized strobe-lights. To find a good landing place, the bat swam around the pond. Anchored in strategic spots my strobe-lights covered most of the area, and a fast

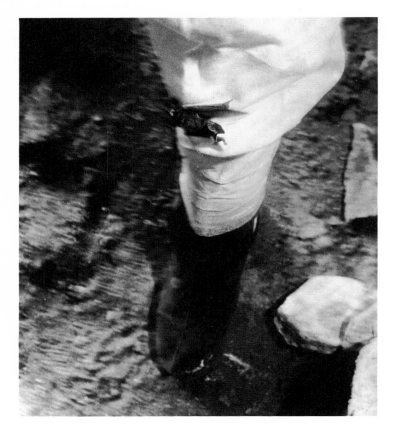

In Bracken Cave a young bat clings to the leg of my jumpsuit.

Bracken Cave. Only small groups of young bats could I see on entering the cave, but somewhere in the darkness were the nurseries I was hoping to find. After a small entrance plateau the cave goes down, deeper and deeper—and this is where the bat mothers prefer to have their babies.

The ground was covered with guano. It felt like walking in deep, dark sand. But one thing is sure: it is much more pleasant to slide down in sand than guano. The big rocks on the way down are mostly covered with mites and it is not advisable to hold on to them. I was never athletic-minded and my first reaction was to survey the terrain from the little plateau. I saw many, many young bats but very few newly born pink babies, and those are the ones I wanted. There was no other choice than to look for them deeper in the cave.

The platform at the entrance was our headquarters where I could unpack my cameras and lights. Many babies were falling from the rocks overhead and tried to crawl up on everything, including my equipment. I put them back on rocks as often as I could but I knew they did not have much chance of survival.

While I was unpacking, Dr. Winkler with Bill and Dennis went down deeper into the cave to find the youngest babies with nursing mothers. When they had found the right spot, I followed. It was quite a way down but I was determined to get there and stay until I had taken my

change to a longer lens made it possible for me to get several different sequences. Anyhow, I was able to take it in Texas without traveling thousands of miles—and the swimming would not have been different in Australia.

In July, 1967, Dr. W. G. Winkler of the South Western Rabies Investigation Station, New Mexico, met me in San Antonio, Texas, to drive with me to Bracken Cave on the following morning. It was late in the season but in a maternity cave of this size (population 15-20 million) there would still be enough babies for me to photograph.

Dr. Winkler and his two associates, Dennis Stubblefield and Bill Adams, called for me at my motel in the morning. They handed me a white jumpsuit to put on over my clothing. My boots were taped tightly to the suit; also taped were the cuffs and neck. I am sure I looked unusual walking through the motel lobby. The reason for this protection is the presence of tiny mites and dermestid beetles in unmeasurable quantities inside the cave. They fall from the ceiling and are everywhere.

We entered the cave. I had never been in a maternity cave before and did not know what conditions to expect. There are many such caves where pictures of baby bats can be taken a few feet from the entrance—but not in

Inside Bracken Cave. The white X's mark the locations of the nurseries I photographed. One is over a small ledge around the bend. (Dr. Winkler and his associates are in the picture.)

166

pictures. To make this trip more than once was out of the question! Dr. Winkler was less concerned about my agility than about my breathing inside the cave. Supposedly two men had died from inhaling ammonia and carbon dioxide in this cave. I had had my rabies injection and after working with animals for years I was not worried about the air. Very confidently I assured Dr. Winkler that I could endure any air for as long as I had to. My problem was the guano: my light stands sank or slid in the soft ground, and as a matter of fact, so did I. Taking with me only one camera with two small synchronized strobelights, I braced one foot against a rock to keep my balance. Dennis was holding my lights in the direction of my shooting (I gave up light stands). It was dark and my only focusing light was the headlight on a helmet. I saw several maternity spots and slowly made my way toward them. Each of them had different, interesting details—I was shooting and didn't think of the passing time.

It seemed to get hotter, and I was thankful for the "wind" the bats made flying back and forth inside the cave. Changing film in the camera got more and more difficult. It had not been easy under these conditions before, but now I could do it only in slow motion. Suddenly I felt that my lungs were *empty*, that I had nothing to breathe with—which may not be a good description of a feeling which cannot be described. I looked up to the cave entrance but it seemed as far as the moon. It took strong arms to help me up to the plateau. Dr. Winkler knew the first-aid treatment and soon I was recuperating at the entrance. I repeatedly told Dr. Winkler how sorry I was to cause trouble and it was wonderful to hear that many men succumbed to the tainted air much faster than I did.

My crushed ego started to inflate again. I didn't want to leave the cave, and decided to wait for the evening exit of the bat mothers. In the late afternoon the sun was still shining when the first signs of the departure were apparent. I expected several million bats to fly out of the cave over my head and was prepared to take pictures, but when they really flew out in full force the spectacle was so unique that I nearly stopped shooting—only a person standing in the way of several million flying bats would understand this. Because bats leave the cave in three shifts, with a pause in between, I had time to find a spot overlooking the cave entrance to shoot the exodus from outside. It was strange to see bats flying in bright sunlight towards the blue sky; this is something you expect only birds to do.

In art, it is an established tradition that when bats are pictured a full moon is shown in the night sky behind them. This night I was sorry the moon was not full, but a half moon was better than none. I stayed as long as there was light enough to take color pictures using fast exposures.

In the light of a pale moon bats were still emerging from the cave hours after they started.

Sometimes I wonder what it means to observe bats "in nature." It is easy to understand what nature means for tigers, bears, giraffes and many other animals: it means jungles, forests, African plains or Australian bush country, wherever animals live in freedom. Bats live there too, but they also live free in houses, churches, farms and attics, even in a corner of a porch in Arizona. They select their caves, trees, rocks or manmade structures and make their "homes." Nobody can tell them where they should live— their "nature" is the cave and the attic.

I could not depend on many picturesque ponds and manmade caves and I did not see much behavior in small, bare wire cages the captured bats so often inhabit. They either hang on the wire or come down to the feeding dish—a dull existence! Thinking about it, I decided to design collapsible, portable cages, with a miniature replica of a bat "home" inside. It was not necessary for them to be masterpieces in landscaping as long as they pleased the bats. I had observed that bats can fly in surprisingly small spaces comparative to their wing spread, smaller than I expected after reading about their flight ability. It meant that the cage did not have to be oversized—very convenient if it had to fit in a car or fly with me as my baggage.

When my cages were ready they solved many of my photographic problems. Made out of wood and chicken-wire, they are easy to assemble. Any background can be

With no glass between us, one of the *Hipposideros* took off in my direction. We both avoided a collision.

taped inside, but it has to be a tight fit, for the smallest opening is enough to let a bat disappear behind the background. On both sides of the cage I can cut out "windows" in the background for my strobe-lights. Over the wire top of the cage I can place the third strobe-light. To prevent the bats from hanging on the cage ceiling, I have to fasten a sheet of plastic inside under the wire. The glass in front is removable and I can shoot with or without it, depending on the situation. While I was shooting without glass the fight of the *Hipposideros* shown in this book, one of the fighters suddenly decided to leave the scene and flew out of the cage. But he couldn't fly out of the room and was soon returned to the branch. Learning from experience, I shot their fighting, from then on, through glass.

Photographing through glass had one bothersome drawback—the reflections. To avoid them everything facing the glass had to be black. I always had lots of black material or black paper with me to cover walls, tables or whatever had to be covered. If there was too much to cover, a black screen I made was placed behind me. All chrome parts of my cameras I covered with black tape. The tripod presented a problem, because tape would have to be removed each time the legs were to be shortened or lengthened. The best solution I could find was to drape black fabric around the tripod, long enough to cover the pulled-out legs. My black working cloth, scarf, sometimes black gloves, camouflaged me nearly perfectly.

168

My theory—that when certain conditions are created, bats would adopt their new home and continue their private life—seemed to be right. For each bat, depending on origin, I tried to get the "nature" as authentic as possible. It was important for the bat's behavior; they clearly liked some tree branches, plants or rocks and disliked others. One of the best examples was the experience with *Euderma*, the spotted bat. When Dr. James Findley of the University of New Mexico phoned me that he had a *Euderma*, I rushed with my cage and equipment to the airport. So little is known about this rare bat that landscaping could only be a guess. The first try was a pine tree branch—pine trees grow in her region—but it was obviously a wrong choice. The little bat moved awkwardly between the branches and did look unhappy and very much out of place. Dr. Findley suggested a lava rock. We substituted the rock for the pine and the difference in behavior was astounding. The bat moved all over the rock, exploring every crevice. It was clear that she felt "at home." After a while she became very quiet, not moving around any more. I worried that she might be dying. On the assumption that she was looking for insects and could be hungry, she was gently offered a mealworm. I was happy to see how readily it was accepted—and about 14 more. The little bat must have been starved. After this hearty meal she discovered a cave in the lava rock, and seemingly content, went inside to sleep. When I saw the color film, I was surprised how perfectly camouflaged the *Euderma* bat was on this lava rock—her colors of gray, white and pink were also in the structure of the rock.

Cynopterus, hanging on a twig, is introduced into a miniature jungle. The bat carefully chose her own place to rest.

For some bats a Lilliputian jungle had to be created, with plants from Asia, West Indies, or other places around the world. With sympathetic help from the New York Botanical Gardens, I was sure to use the right plants for certain geographic locations. Placing lights for a jungle shot isn't easy. I never knew where the bat would be and many times a leaf between the light and the bat caused a minor catastrophe and the whole light arrangement had to be changed. If the bat moved again, the lights moved

My curious friend.

again. It would not help at all to get impatient! Even more trying was sitting and waiting for something which might or might not happen. I got used to long hours of sitting almost motionlessly facing the motionless bats. The red light did not change their biological clock; many bats started to get active only at their own time. With new arrivals I considered the time difference—when night came on where they came from, because it would be the time they might be getting hungry. Patience was most important in all kinds of unexpected confrontations.

For me to get good pictures, the bats had to get used to my presence and consider me a harmless bystander. Sometimes they did show mild interest in me, but in one case it went too far. One old (he looked old to me) vampire appeared from wherever he had been in the cave, to look at me as closely as the glass between us allowed. For close-ups I used a micro lens and had sometimes to bend down to the cave floor level. He found it most interesting to look directly into the lens, preventing me from taking anything. If he would have been a good-looking vampire (there is such a thing), I would have gladly taken his

picture, since he was always available, but with his small eyes, shaggy fur and bleached-out color, he was not photogenic! I had had similar experiences with other animals being attracted by lenses, but somehow it was unexpected with a vampire bat.

The Biology Department of Yale University had a good bat collection and Dr. Alvin Novick allowed me to work in a room specially constructed for bats in the Kline Biology Tower. One day Dr. Novick told me about *Macrotus* hunting big moths and suggested getting some to see if the *Macrotus* would attack them. Most big moths were "out of season," and I felt lucky to wind up with several *Polyphemus* moths which had been hatched by mistake at Yale. (I never found out why it happened.) For two nights I watched and shot some bat-moth encounters. I could not see clearly in the red light, but knew that something was going on. When I looked through the developed film I was surprised to see so many moths "fainting."

Dr. Novick's advice was to show those pictures to Dr. K. D. Roeder of Tuft's University, the authority on echolocation in moths, and ask his opinion. I was stunned when Dr. Roeder took one look at the moth and told me that of all moths I could have photographed, *Polyphemus* is one of the few that have no ears and could not hear the bat's signals. He didn't think that I should take the bat-moth pictures out of my planned book because of scientific opinion today—the scientist may think differently about the *Polyphemus* moth tomorrow.

To be able to evaluate the moth's behavior, Dr. Roeder asked to see the pictures preceding and following the ones I had showed him. I had to confess that I not only didn't have them with me but would hardly know how to find them. I never had the experience before of shooting sequences with possible scientific value and did not realize how important it is to leave those sequences undisturbed. Looking for the best single pictures, I did disturb every possible continuity! I knew that I had to find the right sequences out of hundreds of mixed-up rejects of this take. When I was shooting these pictures part of the film was not transported in the camera. (It wasn't my fault!) At the time it was heartbreaking, because I was sure that my best pictures were among the missing, and maybe they were, but now, sorry to admit, I was glad: for days, assorting mountains of film, I had to match frames to reconstruct the original continuity, until I finally found the missing links to complete the bat-moth sequence. This task would have been easier if the pictures had been taken faster than two in one second. Too much time elapsed between frames to make many of the sequences convincing.

At the time a 35 mm Hulcher camera was being constructed for me with special new features I requested. Mr. Hulcher was willing to make the innovations but warned that it would take longer than the usual several months, the time it takes to make each of his cameras. To be able to shoot with his strobe-lights up to twenty synchronized exposures in one second was so important that I gladly agreed to wait.

One of my ambitions was to take color pictures of *Noctilio*, the fisherman bat, actually catching fish. In nature they fly over water mostly on moonless nights in highly unphotogenic conditions. A giant screened enclosure was built for me in the catacombs of the Bronx Zoo. I had my Hulcher and everything else ready to start the shooting—except the fisherman bats. One day, after months of trying in vain to import *Noctilio*, I got the news that H. B. House, Curator of Mammals in the Bronx Zoo, had returned from Brazil with ten *Noctilio*. They were established in my screened enclosure where roosting places were built for them. The question now was, will they fish? There were water and fish waiting for them— but it wasn't Brazil. Long plane trips are not the best way to travel for bats. This time, being well cared for, they survived. When a call came from Brad House I was glad to hear that all the bats were doing well and busy fishing.

The next day, standing outside their enclosure, I was tensely watching their roosts. Any moment now they might start fishing. Some bats left the roost and flew low over the water, but that's all they did. Slightly disappointed, I decided to cut my first visit short and started to walk away. Suddenly, I heard Brad House's voice triumphantly announce, "They are fishing like mad!" I hurried back, the red light was off, everything was pitch dark and silent but then every few seconds I could hear water splashing and something that sounded like chomping. It was exciting, but invisible. When the red light was switched on there was not a trace of the happenings a moment ago in the darkness. It looked as if the bats didn't even move from their roost.

At this moment, I foresaw what would happen when I would have to move inside the enclosure with cameras and lights and expect them to go on fishing. My thoughts were gloomy and I was right. There was very little space inside for me to keep out of their way. The power-supply cases feeding the strobes, the strobe-lights themselves, the Hulcher motor's separate battery had to be protected from water, wet sand covering the ground and any possible water splashes. I was surrounded by all this electrical equipment and any mishap could be quite dangerous. As with other bats I knew that they had to get used to my presence but in this situation, to expect the bats to ignore me was not realistic—I was anticipating a long trial time.

It took about three to four hours each time to make all preparations for the shooting—connecting wires, placing all units and lights, arranging a dry place for me, etc. Everything had to be ready by 8 p.m. The bats were most active around 11 p.m. From 8 to 11, I had to stay inside, as motionless as I could be in a most uncomfortable position. Three hours seemed to be an excessively long time to wait for the 11 o'clock feeding, but it really wasn't. The bats started flying (not fishing) early in the evening, making short trips from roost to roost at intervals sometimes as long as thirty minutes. I wanted at this time to be stationed to avoid any later disruptions. Needless to say that my best intentions and preparations did not impress the bats—they did not fish. Before I left at night, without fishing pictures, all equipment had to be removed and packed (the removing was much faster than the setting up) until the next try.

There were many, many of those frustrating tries until some bats dared to fish in my presence. Even then new problems came up—the fish had to be gaffed with a claw nearest to me and transferred to the mouth in my direction. Shooting ten, fifteen and sometimes twenty frames in a second and having a fishing sequence did not do any good if a fish did not look like a fish, or if the bat turned away from the camera. There was no way to arrange that; it was luck and an exercise in unlimited patience. I tried and tried till I got it.

I could not observe and photograph many interesting species though I still hope someday to take pictures of a live white bat. To get a complete record in color of bat behavior was a dream I would not think of dreaming...

After three years of photographing bats, I found out that with each new bat came new demands, experimentations and the same old frustrations. It is difficult to remember technical data after months or years had passed (I often can't remember an exposure five minutes after shooting and I never stop to write it down)—but in taking those pictures every success and failure was too important to forget.

—N. L.

ACKNOWLEDGMENTS

When I sat down to write this "Thank You" note to those who helped me I discovered that, unlike my earlier problems on the project, this one was unsolvable. How could I name *every* person? It was impossible to do it right, it was obvious that there was no ideal compromise, and so the best solution was to list those who helped me with locations, bats, advice, literature and, always badly needed, moral support. I have not listed the names in any special order.

Life's Editors with comforting trust encouraged me to continue when the going was rough. The cooperation of *Life's* Color Laboratory was invaluable.

It is impossible for me to name all the students, photo assistants and zoo keepers who worked long hours with me —but I can assure them all that I am very grateful.

I am grateful for everything the following people did to help:

E. LENDELL COCKRUM, Director of the Desert Biology Station of the University of Arizona;

JAMES FINDLEY of the University of New Mexico;

DONALD R. GRIFFIN, Director of the Institute for Research in Animal Behavior of the New York Zoological Society and Rockefeller University;

JACK BRADBURY of the William Beebe Tropical Research Station in Trinidad;

ALVIN NOVICK of Yale University;

W. O'DELL HANSEN of Yale Medical School;

K. D. ROEDER of Tufts University;

BENNY CONSTANTIN of the Naval Biological Laboratory in California;

KARL KOOPMAN of The American Museum of Natural History in New York City;

JOSEPH A. DAVIS, JR., Scientific Assistant to the Director of the New York Zoological Society;

H. B. HOUSE, Curator of Mammals of the New York Zoological Park;

JOHN WERLER, Director, and BOB DOOLY, Curator, of the Houston Zoological Gardens;

EDWARD J. MARUSKA, General Curator of the Cincinnati Zoo;

FRED WEBSTER of Harvard University;

HOWARD A. BALDWIN of the Sensory System Laboratory in Arizona;

ARTHUR M. GREENHALL of the Food and Agricultural Organization of the United Nations in Mexico;

JOHN BORIN of the New York Botanical Gardens;

W. G. WINKLER of the U.S. Public Health Service.

—N. L.

PRODUCTION EDITA S.A.

Editorial supervision by JAY GOLD

Plates, composition and lithography by
Imprimeries Réunies S. A. Lausanne
Binding by Maurice Busenhart, Lausanne

Manufactured in Switzerland